"This is so much more than a math book. It's about a kindergarten teacher who is confident in her teaching, passing on sensible suggestions and practical advice to others who are looking to create interesting, engaging learning environments for their children, outside and in. It contains nuggets of commentary that are an inspiration and a joy to read. It's a reflective narrative of how Deanna integrates math into her everyday life of the class in meaningful and respectful ways based upon the principles and practice of the Reggio Emilia approach."

—JULIET ROBERTSON, author of *Messy Maths:*
A Playful, Outdoor Approach for Early Years

"In this beautiful book, Deanna McLennan shows us how teachers can create an environment for children to engage in mathematical play and learning with joy, curiosity, and discovery. Teachers will welcome these wonderfully authentic invitations to bring joyful, playful math into their classrooms throughout the day."

—KATIE KEIER, kindergarten teacher and co-author of
Catching Readers Before They Fall: Supporting
Readers Who Struggle, K–4

"Deanna shows us that math can bring joy! Written to support play-based math learning for young children in clear and concise language, this colorfully illustrated text is all you need to give the gift of math to children. When math is connected to children's play it becomes real, meaningful, authentic, and joyful for children and their teachers."

—DR. DIANE KASHIN, RECE, retired early childhood education professor,
co-author of *Play and Learning in Early Childhood Education*

"What if all children had joyful math experiences in their earliest years? You may be wondering *what would that look like and where do I start*. Read *Joyful Math* and step inside Deanna McLennan's masterful, joy-filled kindergarten classroom. Here the natural curiosity, inventiveness, and exuberance of children is harnessed for deep mathematical learning through exploration and play. Deanna respectfully shares with teachers the methods she has developed over the years to surpass mathematical standards without leaving joy to chance. Rich with stories, conversations with children, and awe-inspiring photographs, *Joyful Math* is a game-changer for the early childhood math landscape."

—KATIE EGAN CUNNINGHAM, author of *Start with Joy: Designing Literacy Learning for Student Happiness*

"Deanna's book provides a window into an early childhood classroom, sharing stories of young children's mathematics learning. The mathematics is embedded in a place of wonder, joy, and collaboration, full of playful learning with materials. The classroom stories share a joyful approach to the teaching and learning of mathematics which is sure to both inspire and provide a wealth of ideas for educators."

—JANICE NOVAKOWSKI, District Teacher Consultant (Mathematics) in Richmond, BC, Canada and coordinator of the BC Reggio-Inspired Mathematics Project

Joyful Math

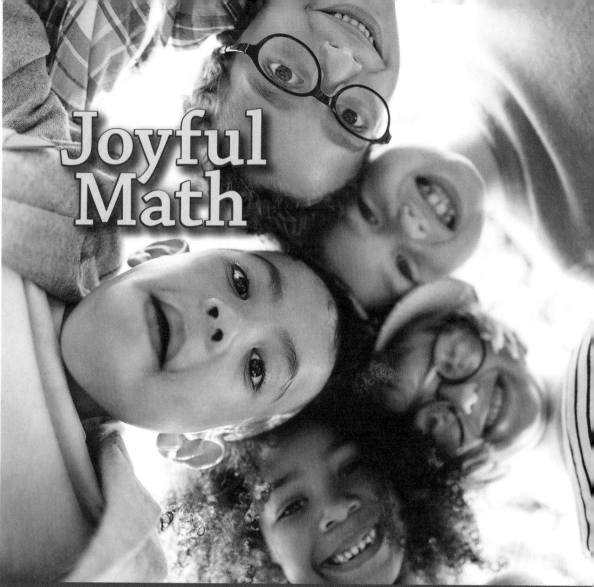

Joyful Math

Invitations to Play and Explore in the
Early Childhood Classroom

DEANNA PECASKI McLENNAN

Stenhouse
PUBLISHERS

www.stenhouse.com

PORTSMOUTH, NEW HAMPSHIRE

Stenhouse Publishers
www.stenhouse.com

Library of Congress Cataloging-in-Publication Data
Names: McLennan, Deanna Pecaski, author.
Title: Joyful math : invitations to play and explore in the early childhood
    classroom / Deanna Pecaski McLennan.
Description: Portsmouth, New Hampshire : Stenhouse Publishers, [2020] |
    Includes bibliographical references. |
Identifiers: LCCN 2019049440 (print) | LCCN 2019049441 (ebook) | ISBN
    9781625313256 (paperback) | ISBN 9781625313263 (ebook)
Subjects: LCSH: Mathematics—Study and teaching (Early childhood)
Classification: LCC QA135.6 .M395 2020 (print) | LCC QA135.6 (ebook) |
    DDC 372.7/049—dc23
LC record available at https://lccn.loc.gov/2019049440
LC ebook record available at https://lccn.loc.gov/2019049441

Cover design and interior design Jill Shaffer
Typesetting by Eclipse Publishing Services

Manufactured in the United States of America

 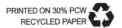
26 25 24 23 22 21 20   9 8 7 6 5 4 3 2 1

For Trevor
who fills my life with joy and love

Contents

Acknowledgments

WRITING A BOOK is not an easy task. This project would not have been possible without the love, support, and guidance of many special people in my life.

To my husband, Trevor, thank you for your never-ending belief in my work. You are always there with support and encouragement, and ready to help out however you can. To my three children, Cadence, Caleb, and Quinn, thank you for helping me see the world through joyful eyes. So much of who I am as an educator and mother is because of what you have taught me. I love our adventures and am so proud that you are mine.

To my parents, Antoinette and Ernest Pecaski, thank you for always being there for me. My life has been beautifully shaped by the amazing childhood you provided. I couldn't ask for more encouraging, supportive parents. Anthony and Dana, thank you for your never-ending cheerleading! Your interest in my educational pursuits and supportive words were appreciated more than you know.

Extended family has played an important role in my life as well. Tom and Marita, Ken and Liz, and Scott and Amanda, thank you for helping out however you could to support my work. Inquiring about how things were going, celebrating my publications over the years, and cheering for me from the sidelines always drove me forward.

To the many wonderful children, families, administrators, and colleagues I've had the incredible pleasure of working with each day, thank you! I want nothing more than to be the best educator I can be for you. I want the children in my care to develop as happy, confident, and capable mathematicians—for the future of our world lies safely in their hands.

Kassia Wedekind, I cannot thank you enough for believing in my work, taking a chance on me, and encouraging me to transform my ideas into a book. Your critical and caring eyes have helped me reflect deeply upon my pedagogy and practice. To the editing and production team at Stenhouse, thank you for your dedicated work on this project. A special thanks to Lynne Costa, Shannon St. Peter, Jay Kilburn, Faye LaCasse, Jill Backman, and Lisa Sullivan..

Thank you to artists Rebecca Bayer and David Gregory for allowing me to use a photo of their beautiful and mathematical series of tile mosaics, *The Whole Is Greater Than the Sum of Its Parts*. These mosaic panels are inspiring to all who pass through the Sherbourne station of the Toronto subway.

And finally, I wish to thank my grandmothers, Carmela DeThomasis and Mary Pecaski. I was blessed to grow into adulthood with two loving, supportive grandmothers who took pride in all I accomplished. Although neither is still with me, their love of family, life, and storytelling continue to inspire. They live on through the words I write each day.

CHAPTER 1

Discovering the Joy in Math

T he sound of Charlie's laughter could be heard from anywhere in the schoolyard. I always knew immediately where to look. There he was racing a green tractor in the middle of a giant puddle.

"Look, Mrs. McLennan! Look at me! My truck is so fast! I am making huge waves! They are going to be bigger than my boots!"

I smiled. No one captured the exuberant joy of childhood like Charlie. He lived for imaginary play with trucks and was rarely seen without one in hand. No matter how long Charlie spent outside, when he heard the call to head indoors he would run to the closest puddle and race his truck through the water one more time, relishing every last splash. The amount of mud on his clothing was a measure of the joy Charlie experienced with his truck play.

FIGURE 1.1
A child explores the process of moving rocks of different sizes in a toy truck.

REFLECT UPON your own life as you think about Charlie's love of imaginary play. What are you most passionate about? What drives you deeply in your professional work? What feels like play to you? For Charlie, it didn't matter if it was hot or cold, dry or muddy. Nothing stopped him from enjoying his time playing with trucks. Adverse weather conditions only drove Charlie further in his explorations. Too much mud in the schoolyard? His truck transformed into a mighty machine that could easily cut through the muck. Snowy conditions? His truck would help clear a path for us to walk through. Lots of rain that day? No problem! He was dressed for the weather. He once measured how much fun he had by how much water he could empty from his boot: "I had so much fun today my *entire boot* got filled." Like Charlie, each of us has something we feel deeply about that drives us to be the best educators we can be. Take a moment to think about the special interests and talents you bring to your teaching practice. How do these shape your classroom into a positive and productive place that makes everyone inside feel inspired in their interactions and learning together?

Now think about math. What is your initial reaction? Did you smile? Cringe? Sigh? Think back to your previous experiences with math. What is your happiest math memory? Most frustrating? Perhaps math is something you already enjoy, and you are reading this book because you are inspired to learn more. Or maybe math is something that fills you with anxiety, and you are caught between wishing you could avoid it altogether and wanting your students' math experiences to be more positive than your own.

Math is something that brings me great joy—it's my favorite area to explore with my kindergarten students, and I tend to look at everything in my teaching practice through a mathematical lens. When I think about math, I feel curious and engaged. I want to learn as much as I can and grow my mathematical understanding and mindset in order to help my students grow theirs. Some people read fictional fantasies to relax after a long week of work. I pour myself a glass of wine and read math books for fun. When I'm engaged in math teaching and learning, I feel that same playful joy that Charlie experiences when he splashes through a muddy puddle with his truck. But it wasn't always this way for me.

As a child I enjoyed school. I liked parameters and rules and knowing exactly what I had to do in order to be successful. I got good grades because I delivered exactly what my teachers expected on tests and assignments—correct answers. Math worksheets were especially fulfilling for me in the primary grades—the predictable rhythm of plugging numbers into equations and writing rows of answers appealed to my love of order and task completion. I remember being thrilled in second grade because I got to bring home a half-filled workbook for the summer. Nothing pleased me more than seeing check marks all over my page and receiving the most coveted prize of all—a sticker sparkling on the top of the worksheet communicating my achievement for all to see.

However, as I grew older, my relationship with math began to change. Memorizing formulas and copying the teacher's models helped me keep my grades up, but I didn't really understand the reasoning behind the symbols. I worried endlessly that I would not know the answers to my teacher's questions and be discovered as a math fraud. I still recall slumping in my seat in my seventh-grade classroom, covering a high grade on my test with my hand because I was worried that I would be called on to explain my answers to the class. I had memorized enough procedures to do well on the test, but the idea of being called on to explain my thinking shot a surge of fear through my body.

The experience that finally ended all hope for me when it came to school math was my twelfth-grade algebra class. Each day our teacher would write students' names next to numbers on the board so that when we entered the room, we knew which homework questions we were responsible for sharing. My dread of that experience would begin at lunch and increase in intensity until I arrived in algebra class for fourth period. Every day, as I entered the classroom, my stomach was knotted with worry that it would be my turn to share. It wasn't because I hadn't done the homework. I just didn't understand the math, and I wasn't sure where to begin in trying to explain it. I hated the idea of putting my work out there for everyone to deconstruct. If your answer was wrong, or your thinking didn't make sense, you were met with mocking looks from your peers. This class was not a fun place for anyone to be, especially for a teenager already struggling to develop a sense of self, and worried about social acceptance from her peers.

After that experience I was done with math. I never enrolled in another math course after that point, and with that decision, I ended the possibility of future university math courses or a career in mathematics and sciences. I often look back at that time in my life and wonder "what if?" How differently might my life have unfolded if my teachers had relied less on didactic practices and instead embraced a collaborative approach to learning that focused on understanding? What if we had focused on enjoying and truly comprehending the math as much as getting the answers correct?

After high school I pursued teaching and found my passion in early childhood. In my new career I supported children's math learning the best I could; I followed teacher guides and sought the advice of colleagues. I taught math because it was required, not because I found beauty or inspiration in it. Then one day my oldest child, in the fourth grade at the time, came home from school declaring that she hated math—she didn't understand it, felt uncomfortable with it, and resented that even though she wanted to be better at math, she didn't know how. I was immediately transported back to my twelfth-grade algebra class, and I knew that as an educator I had to do something. Horrified that my daughter and my own young students might follow in my footsteps, I sought change in my own teaching practice. I knew that early childhood environments, like my kindergarten class, offered children rich possibilities to explore in meaningful ways. How could I transform my own classroom into a place where children loved math and appreciated its relationship to their lives and the greater world? How could I help families overcome their past experiences with math and recognize that they had valuable mathematical ideas to offer their children and our classroom? How could math become something we, both teachers and students, wanted to explore in our classroom?

This book is an effort to dig into these questions. Early childhood teachers are experts at following students' interests, providing space to explore, and giving children opportunities to develop ideas over time. This book investigates how we can build on these strengths, helping young children develop mathematical understandings and mindsets through play. In Chapter 2 we consider how the design of our classroom space and environment can foster inquiry and wonder for mathematics. In Chapters 3, 4, and 5 we explore ways to invite children to engage in mathematics through art, outdoor play, and literacy. In Chapter 6 we investigate ways that ongoing documentation can support children's learning and community engagement.

O ne afternoon during choice time, a peal of laughter rang through our classroom. I immediately knew it was Charlie and guessed that he had discovered the new mini-vehicle set I had placed in the building area earlier that morning. I walked over to investigate.

"What are you doing?" I asked him.

"Look at these!" In his hand he held a tiny firetruck and police cruiser. "They are so small! I bet I can fit at least two more in one hand!"

"I wonder how many you could hold in both hands at the same time," I challenged him.

"Well, at least six, because I have three now and then I could hold three more," he responded. Charlie grabbed three more vehicles from the basket and counted aloud. "One, two, three, four, five, six!" He smiled. "When I get bigger, I will be able to hold even more!"

"Why do you think that?" I questioned.

"Because my hands will be even bigger than yours!"

"How many do you think I can hold in one hand now?" I asked.

"Hmm. Maybe four? Your hands are bigger than mine, but not that much bigger. See!" Charlie put his vehicles down in the basket and grabbed one of my hands, holding his palm up to mine. "Yep, I think you can only hold four."

"Okay, let's see if you're right," I challenged. I grabbed a fistful of vehicles, fitting six in one hand.

"Whoa! That's more than I thought! That's how many I can hold in two hands!" Charlie called out to his friend Evan across the room. "Evan! Hey, Evan! Mrs. McLennan can hold six cars in one hand!" Evan walked over to where we were standing.

"I bet I can hold more!" Evan confidently asserted. "My hands are bigger than yours are, Charlie."

"Let's see what you can do!" Charlie pushed the basket toward Evan. And with that simple exchange a playful class competition began—to see who could hold the most mini-vehicles using both hands.

THIS BOOK is filled with vignettes, photos, and ideas gathered from my time exploring math alongside young children. I hope these stories honor the children's work and provide inspiration for teachers. This book is not a math program or handbook with a linear list of "must-dos" that you tick off, hoping they will result in student achievement. Rather, these are the stories of the math learning I've experienced in my classroom over time. I hope they inspire you to embrace math in all its joyful possibilities— to take risks, try different approaches, observe carefully, encourage children to be co-learners with you, and share what you learn beyond the walls of your classroom.

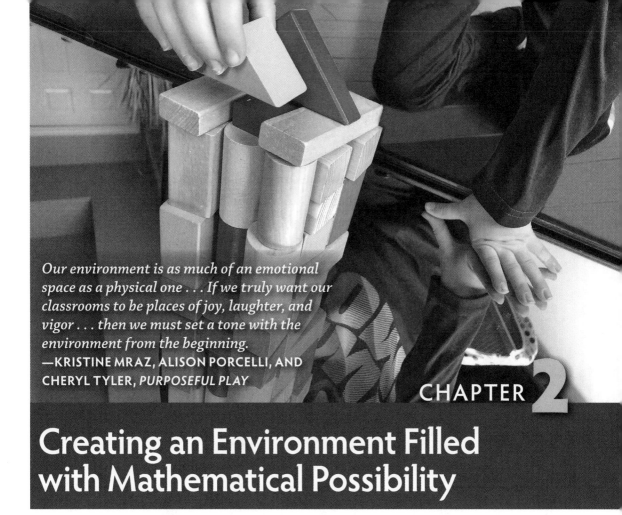

Our environment is as much of an emotional space as a physical one . . . If we truly want our classrooms to be places of joy, laughter, and vigor . . . then we must set a tone with the environment from the beginning.
—KRISTINE MRAZ, ALISON PORCELLI, AND CHERYL TYLER, *PURPOSEFUL PLAY*

CHAPTER 2

Creating an Environment Filled with Mathematical Possibility

FIGURE 2.1
A child builds with wooden blocks on top of a safety mirror.

F elix sat on a pillow in the cozy reading area exploring a book about the CN Tower in Toronto.

"Look how tall it is," he whispered to himself as his finger traced a large black and white photo. "If I was at the top, I could see all of Canada." Felix put the book down and walked over to the building shelf, where he retrieved a basket of blocks. After dragging it back to his pillow, he propped up the book and began to build. Every few minutes he referenced the photo in the book.

"Look! I'm making the CN Tower!" he called out. A few children working in nearby centers stopped what they were doing and moved closer.

"That's not tall enough," critiqued Harper. "I've been to Toronto, and the CN Tower is so tall there are clouds at the top." Felix continued to stack blocks until the basket was empty.

"It's not tall enough," he observed. "I need more blocks."

"There aren't any more," Harper stated as she looked into the basket.

"But how can I make the tower taller?" Felix wondered.

"I know!" piped up Oliver, who had been listening and watching from a nearby center. Oliver ran over to the art center, where he retrieved a safety mirror. "Put this at the bottom!"

Felix laid the mirror next to his tower and gently began to rebuild it, piece by piece, on top of the mirror.

"Hey! When you look down in the mirror, the tower looks like it's going forever!" laughed Oliver. The children stood and stared down, amazed at the way the reflection appeared to double the height of the tower.

"Now it's tall enough!" approved Harper.

THE ENVIRONMENT that surrounds us in the classroom has a tremendous influence on children's learning—from the way children interact with one another and the teachers to the ways in which they engage as readers, writers, mathematicians, and scientists. So, what exactly do we mean when we say "classroom environment"? Julianne Wurm (2005) makes an important distinction between the terms *space* and *environment*: *space* is the physical setup of the classroom, including static features like windows and doors, while *environment* refers to the ways in which the space is used. At its best, classroom environment honors children and the many kinds of knowledge they bring with them into the classroom. It reflects memories of how the children have learned and lived in the classroom together over time and inspires new learning.

The environment in our classroom encouraged Felix to notice and wonder as he browsed the book about the CN Tower, to ask his own question ("How can I build a tall tower like the CN Tower?"), to gather the materials from different areas of the classroom, and to collaborate with others to revise his ideas as he built with the blocks. This kind of classroom culture and environment that support mathematical play and thinking are not achieved by chance but, rather, are carefully co-planned and revised together by teachers and children. Each year looks a little different as teachers balance the children's interests with the curriculum, always aspiring to encourage mathematical curiosity and problem solving through the decisions we make within our classroom spaces.

Starting the Year with a Blank Canvas

ON THE FIRST few days of school, our classroom is a blank canvas. The shelves offer a few basic materials that are familiar, open-ended, and inviting (e.g., construction paper, crayons, markers, scissors), and there is no artwork or documentation displayed yet on our walls (see Figures 2.2 and 2.3). When preparing the classroom space, I try to remember who it is truly intended for. I resist pressure to have the classroom "picture perfect" for the children. Instead I want the children's curiosities and interests to drive our work and our space forward.

During those first few weeks of school, after the children have arrived and are comfortable working within the space, we build the environment together and revise it continually throughout the year to serve our needs. The children are co-creators of almost every space in some way, from the

FIGURE 2.2
An empty writing center at the beginning of the school year before it is co-constructed with children.

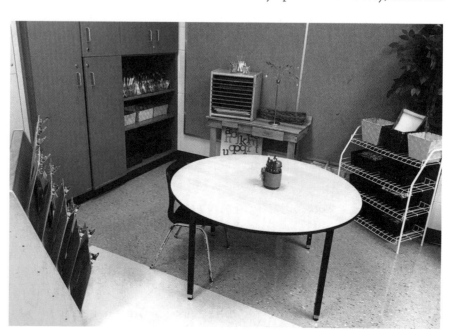

FIGURE 2.3
*A garden trellis
and mini-easels
wait to be filled
with student
artwork and
documentation.*

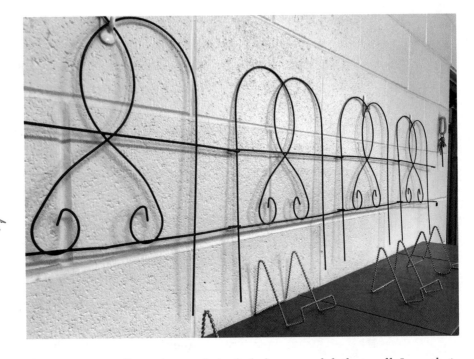

charts on our walls to the words included on our alphabet wall. I use their interests to choose the books I read aloud at whole-group time, and I fill bulletin boards with their artwork, photos, and drawings. Children offer suggestions for how to organize materials in each area and work together to organize displays of their creations. I add photos of the children and typed teacher narrative so that documentation is present around the classroom. As children discover new ideas, we add representations of these ideas to areas throughout the classroom to enhance learning. For example, when children experimented with mixing the primary colors, the recipes they created for making secondary colors were added to the art area; when children became interested in high-frequency words, they wrote them on index cards, sorted them by the number of letters in each word, and created reference rings for use at the writing center; after children researched a number of different plants in our schoolyard, we created a book on that topic and added it to the classroom library.

A principle of the Reggio Emilia approach to early childhood education is that the environment is the "third teacher" (with families and educators being the other two). The environment is the canvas on which educators and children create and reflect upon shared experiences (Wurm 2005). This idea of the environment as the third teacher can help shape the decisions that we, as teachers, make about the classroom environment. How can the choices we make about the space around us empower students as mathematical thinkers? How can we use the space to inspire children's new ideas as well as encourage them to reflect on and revise their current ideas? How can we invite families and the local community to engage with our classroom community in ways that inspire mathematical thinking?

Step Inside Our Classroom

FIGURE 2.4
Fresh flowers picked from a community garden brighten the learning space while inspiring children to draw still life pictures.

SO, WHAT DO these ideas about classroom environment look like, sound like, and feel like in practice? Let's take a peek into my own classroom and deconstruct the decisions the students and I have made about our space. Of course, every school, classroom, and group of teachers and students are unique. Even the space within the four walls of my own classroom has evolved and looked different from year to year. The goal is not to duplicate the decisions I have made in my classroom but, rather, to reflect on the choices we have within our environment and consider the ways that environment influences mathematical exploration.

The choices we make about our classroom environment are guided by our beliefs about how children learn. Here are some of the beliefs that have guided the decisions I have made in my classroom. As you read through them, consider which of these ideas

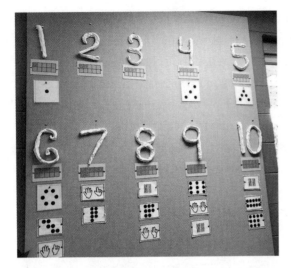

are most important to you and which beliefs you would add to this list.

◆ Children are capable of constructing meaningful ideas.

◆ Children form an understanding of themselves and their place in the world through their interactions with others.

◆ Children are effective communicators.

◆ The environment is a teacher and can inspire thinking and collaboration.

◆ The adults in the room are co-learners, mentors, and guides.

◆ Documenting children's thinking honors their ideas and helps them build upon their understandings.

◆ Children's families and communities can be represented and honored in different ways throughout the classroom.

FIGURE 2.5
Different representations of quantities are displayed on a number wall in the classroom. As children discover different ways of representing numbers (e.g., tallies, ten frames, fingers, dots), these are added underneath the corresponding number.

FIGURE 2.6
After children spent time exploring different shades and tints of color, they sorted and strung similarly colored beads and buttons. These creations were then displayed in a classroom window.

FIGURE 2.7
Children sorted and organized loose parts by size, color, and material. These collections were kept on a window ledge so they could be illuminated by the morning sun.

A NOTE ABOUT CHOICE TIME

While we have dedicated time for math in our schedule each day, I want my students to understand that math does not exist only within a tightly confined time and space in our school day. Throughout this book, many of the math experiences you will read about occur during outdoor play time and daily choice time. During choice time, children work and play in purposefully designed centers throughout the classroom. During this time, I confer with individual students and groups of students about their ideas—asking questions and gently nudging children to consider new ideas, many of them mathematical.

In our classroom, choice time begins after a morning circle time, during which I introduce students to new activities, tools, and materials available throughout the classroom. During this circle time, we may also briefly discuss ideas children have for the new activities and talk about practical matters such as caring for and cleaning up materials and tools. During choice time, we also problem solve social issues such as how to manage busier centers and share materials when students have different ideas about how to use them. After choice time, children gather again on our communal carpet for a sharing circle. During this time, I encourage students to share any artifacts from their experiences at the centers (e.g., artwork, block structures, writing) and answer questions from their peers. I also highlight work that I have noticed throughout the morning, often using a smart device and projector to display photos and videos of the children.

While your classroom may not have this exact structure for choice time, providing dedicated time each day for children to investigate their own questions and ideas through play is critical for early childhood classrooms and something we should continually advocate for and work to protect.

Physical Arrangement

OUR CLASSROOM is a large rectangular space with windows on one side. In this space, we have a bathroom as well as cubbies for students to store their belongings as they come in. Even though the physical room has a rigid rectangular perimeter, our classroom revolves around a large circular meeting area in the center (see Figure 2.9). This space includes a carpet on which we can gather as a community. Around the carpet I have organized learning areas—writing, reading, snack, art, science and nature, dramatic arts, sensory (sand and water tables), and loose parts and construction. I imagine our classroom as a circle with the meeting area at the center and all of the other areas connecting to each other and back to our central meeting area. When children are engaged in choice time, they are able to move between the different areas of the classroom, bringing materials from those areas to the central carpet or to a different center, and collaborating with their peers as they explore and investigate.

Here are some of the choice-time spaces we have created throughout our classroom. As you read, consider what mathematical invitations you offer to the students in your classroom and how the materials themselves might invite students to ask and investigate their own mathematical questions.

Writing Center. A variety of materials are available in the writing center, including paper, pencils, crayons, markers, magnet letters, alphabet tracers, and vocabulary cards. Children often come to the writing center during choice time to make a sign about a building they have made with blocks, to write a survey question for their peers, to create their own books based on a book we have read together as a class, or to write a letter to a friend.

FIGURE 2.8
The classroom is warm and inviting, with learning materials available throughout the space.

FIGURE 2.9

An open meeting area allows children to gather for whole-group lessons and activities. It also provides a larger space for exploration with blocks and other building materials.

Reading Center. In the reading center, children can choose to explore and read books or engage in an activity (e.g., alphabet puzzles, calming sensory jars). As in the case of Felix building his own version of the CN Tower, books often inspire children's mathematical play and give them opportunities to think mathematically about both stories and illustrations.

Art Center. Children are invited to use a variety of purchased, found, and repurposed tools and materials to create art. Students take great pride in sorting, grouping, counting, and displaying the available materials. As artists, they engage in many of the same practices as mathematicians, including solving problems, considering tool usage, and revising their ideas. Children consider lines, shapes, space, and quantity from the perspective of both an artist and a mathematician.

Math Center. While we often talk about how math is present everywhere in our classroom and beyond, the math center is an area where special math tools and materials are stored in easy-to-access baskets and containers. Children are invited to explore the resources at a nearby table

FIGURE 2.10
Children have access to a variety of math tools and can integrate them into their play throughout the classroom. As new tools are introduced to children and explored in small-group activities, they are added to the shelf.

or carpet or integrate them into other areas of the classroom. For example, one child in our classroom used a measuring tape to measure the circumference of a friend's head in order to make a hat in the art center. Another child used arrow direction cards to outline a "road" for mini-vehicles in the building center.

Loose Parts Center. Loose parts can include repurposed, found, and natural materials that are easily manipulated by children in exploratory activities (e.g., shells, gems, stones, bottle caps). Children use nearby carpets and tables to engage in activities such as sorting, patterning, counting, and graphing the materials; measuring the area or perimeter of objects (e.g., counting how many shells fill a frame or

FIGURE 2.11
Many collections of natural, repurposed, and found loose parts are available in the loose parts center. Families are invited to collect materials from their yards and neighborhoods and donate these to the classroom.

calculating how many rocks are needed to go around the perimeter of a carpet space); and creating symmetrical designs.

FIGURE 2.12
Children naturally incorporate mathematics in the dramatic arts center through their imaginative play.

Dramatic Arts Center. In this area children engage in sociodramatic play scenarios in which they can role-play and explore familiar and unfamiliar situations (e.g., house, restaurant, vet office, store). Children can plan and co-create the space together with a teacher so that it is realistic and inviting for play. The math that comes up in this center often depends on the context of the play. For example, children might follow the directions of a recipe while "cooking" in the kitchen; they might dial numbers on the phone to make an appointment at the doctor's office; or they might accept play money and make change at a florist shop, writing a receipt for how much a flower arrangement costs.

Building Center. The building center is a large area of the classroom where children have space to plan and build large structures using a variety of materials, including blocks, train tracks, ramps, and tubes. Big body activities such as stacking blocks into tall towers, laying on the carpet while racing cars, and designing an elaborate train track require coordination and cooperation. Many math experiences emerge through building opportunities. Children engage in problem solving to create a tall tower that doesn't topple or a bridge that can hold many cars; they explore symmetry while creating aesthetically pleasing designs; or they discuss the shape and size of famous structures and replicate them on a small scale.

Light Play Center. This center is perfect for a classroom nook or corner away from windows and other light sources. Projectors, flashlights, light tables, and other intriguing machines that make light can be placed here. Children are invited to use materials from around the classroom, especially loose parts, to play with color, shadow, and shape. Children may consider the reflection of a shadow on the wall while playing with familiar objects on an overhead projector; they may notice and name the creation of new colors when translucent film is layered on a light panel; or they may see how shadows change when a light source is moved further away from an object.

Snack Center. Students in our classroom eat snacks at various times throughout our choice time. The designated snack table is equipped with napkins and extra forks and spoons and located near the garbage and recycling containers. Children eat when they are hungry and learn how to clean up after themselves and care for the space. Teachers can create opportunities for math talk during snack by placing an easel nearby with a survey question of the day to which the children respond. Teachers might write the question of the day at the beginning of the year and then later invite children to come up with their own questions.

Small World Center. These playscapes can be created ahead of time by a teacher and placed in a sensory bin or on a table. Children can also help co-create these scenarios as interests in different living things (e.g., ladybugs, puppies, worms) emerge in conversations. Twigs, moss, pebbles, shells, and other interesting objects create the setting, and small toys and manipulatives (e.g., plastic spiders, small farm animals) are added for children to manipulate and use while telling stories. Children expand their language by telling stories together and mathematizing their play.

Sensory Bins. Large, deep sensory bins filled with inviting materials (e.g., sand, beads, dried beans or pasta, water) and placed in an easy-to-clean area are an engaging way for children to explore many math ideas.

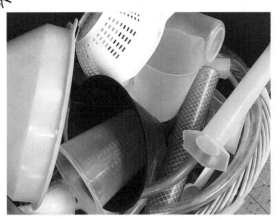

FIGURE 2.13
Repurposed tubes, funnels, cups, spoons, and bowls are available to support children's explorations in the sensory tables indoors and out.

FIGURE 2.14
A child organizes small containers and uses a measuring cup to fill them at the water table.

Adding measuring cups, spoons, funnels, tubes, and other containers to the sensory bins can encourage students to explore measurement, estimation, and counting.

As children engage with materials during choice time, interactions with teachers and peers can help them build upon their prior knowledge, create and clarify new understandings, and experience a variety of approaches to figuring out a question or problem.

Using Invitations and Provocations

A WIDE VARIETY of materials are continually added to our classroom space. Children often contribute by bringing interesting objects from their homes and yards, and I like to share treasures that I find in my personal life as well—items from nature, objects from secondhand stores, souvenirs from travel, and everyday objects that can be used in innovative ways. I like to place these around the room in different centers, sometimes in the middle of a table to be noticed immediately, and other times integrated more deeply in centers for gradual discovery. I strive to create a place that appeals to children's natural curiosity

FIGURE 2.15
A collection of shells and modeling dough flecked with sand invite math exploration as children mold the dough into different shapes and designs, and create prints and patterns using the shells.

about their world; I want them to enter our classroom each day eager to notice the objects I've shared and excited for the experiences that await. Sometimes I purposely display objects in order to encourage curiosity around a particular curriculum standard or concept (e.g., an old scale if I know we are entering a measurement unit, or objects that encourage various ways of exploring numbers). Other times the artifacts are open-ended and whimsical, with no specific outcome in my mind (e.g., an antique kaleidoscope, a rotary phone, an old-fashioned photo). Beverlie Dietze and Diane Kashin (2019) suggest other types of provocations that can lead children to rich

FIGURE 2.16
Many ways to explore numbers are presented to children at the math table.

FIGURE 2.17
An interest in sunflowers inspired art making, as children stamped paint using dried seed heads. The children noticed patterns in the petal and seed formation, leading to an in-depth exploration of patterns in nature.

learning: photos of children engaged in activities from their home and school environments, shared experiences including excursions around the school and field trips into the community, captivating resources such as colorful books or unfamiliar tools, and unique materials that children may have no experience with. If children tire of the materials or do not indicate interest at the initial presentation, then I remove them from the classroom and save them for another time.

Presenting unfamiliar objects to children can also be an effective way to make a connection to a math idea. For example, after reading the book *Caps for Sale* by Esphyr Slobodkina, the students became interested in creating hats using paper and tape. Although they were highly motivated, they struggled to create paper hats that fit their heads properly. The hats were either too big and slid down their faces, or they were too small to fit. We happened to be in the middle of our measurement unit of study, and I wondered how I might help students make connections between the ideas we were exploring in math and their interest in and questions about hats. After showing the children a video of an antique hat-measuring tool, I asked for their input about how we could use familiar tools (e.g., measuring tapes, connecting links) to measure the circumference of our heads and create our own fun hats in the art area.

Other times, I have displayed an interesting object and hoped that authentic math might emerge from the children's observations and questions. After adding a rotary phone to the dramatic arts center, I was

FIGURE 2.18
Large playing cards and a variety of math tools and loose parts invite children to explore how numbers can be represented and composed in many ways.

surprised to see the children become curious about the length of rotation for each number dialed. Having no experience with this type of phone, they needed to research how it worked in real life. They spent much time identifying familiar numbers on the dial and exploring how they could turn it with their fingers. It was clear many children had never seen a rotary phone before. The children worked in pairs, first dialing familiar number patterns (e.g., counting by ones, by twos, backward from ten) and then trying other combinations (e.g., their home phone numbers). As they dialed, they noticed smaller numbers had a shorter rotation time and that this rotation time increased with each number.

FIGURE 2.19
Putting natural objects together with math tools such as number lines, connecting cubes, and links inspires children to explore objects mathematically that they might otherwise not.

FIGURE 2.20
Seasonal holidays can inspire math too. In this invitation children were encouraged to cut lengths of ribbon and use them to string felt hearts.

FIGURE 2.21
Wooden catapults can easily be made by attaching clothespins to blocks with rubber bands. Children can use the catapults to "fire" foam chips into a bowl and then record their results using grid paper.

FIGURE 2.22
Incorporating math invitations in the art center can help children learn new and interesting terms and concepts. Here children explored Möbius strips by turning them into hearts.

The Sound of the Classroom

I heard a commotion and looked across the classroom. Many children were gathered around the water table. Earlier that day containers of food coloring and pipettes had been added to the water table, and this addition was proving to be more popular than I had anticipated. I walked over to get a closer look at what was happening and noticed many children crowded around the perimeter of the sensory bin, frustrated that there weren't enough materials for them to use.

"How are things going at this center?" I asked.

"Not good," replied Craig. "We all want to play, and there isn't enough room."

"Or enough pipettes," Marija added.

"The blue water spilled because someone was fighting over it," Cody shared.

"Hmm. It sounds like more people want to play here than there is space for at the moment. I wonder how we can figure this out. What can we do to make sure everyone gets a fair turn playing here?"

The children shrugged their shoulders. No one answered my question.

"It sounds like everyone wants to be at this center right now, but there isn't enough room. Have you ever wanted a toy that someone else was playing with? How did you solve the problem?"

The children remained silent for a few minutes. I resisted the urge to jump in and solve the problem for them.

Sam spoke up. "At my house, my brother and I always want to watch TV at the same time. When we both want to pick the show, we play rock-paper-scissors to decide."

"That's an interesting idea, Sam. I wonder if that strategy would work here too," I replied.

"At our house, my mom sets a timer on her phone. When it beeps, I have to turn my show off and then my brother gets to decide what to watch," shared Marija.

I acknowledged her idea. "We have timers here too. I bet we could use that same idea for taking turns at the water table."

"Oh! At our house, each person is in charge of the TV for the day. We each get a day, and if it's not your day you have to watch what someone else wants to," Carmela piggybacked on Sam's idea.

"What about writing our names down on a piece of paper. If you want a turn, you sign up and then we go in order?" Pablo gestured toward a nearby easel.

"These are all interesting ideas. Let's pick one to try right now so that everyone can have a turn exploring the new materials at the water table."

IF YOU VISIT our classroom when children are present, you will immediately notice all kinds of talking and listening going on. Children are encouraged to engage in conversations with one another, and the hum of the classroom is indicative of collaborative sharing and learning. Sometimes children work through situations of disagreement, like in the case of the crowded water table. Although I encourage children to use an indoor voice and do monitor noise levels, I also believe that disagreement, laughter, and conversation are indications that children are thinking and exploring together. One of my favorite parts of the day is when I can observe children's conversations and interactions during choice time. During this time, my most important role is that of a listener. Think back to the crowded water table. After the children worked out a system of keeping track of turns at the water table, I stayed for a few minutes watching Evette and Conroy's play.

> **Evette:** Look at this teeny-tiny scoop, Conroy. It's the baby scoop.
> **Conroy:** Use that baby scoop to fill up this big measuring cup.
> **Evette:** That would take a hundred years. Let's use this little cup to fill up the big cup instead.
> **Conroy:** Okay, I think we will need four of those little cups to fill the big one. I'll count. One, two, three. No wait! We will need eight little cups to fill the big one.

Being a listener in this conversation allowed me to better observe the mathematical ideas Evette and Conroy were coming up with as they

FIGURE 2.23
Open spaces are available throughout the classroom for the children to use. Materials can be transported from one area to another with the understanding that children will return the materials to their original location when they are finished using them.

talked with each other and interacted with the water table. The two children explored big ideas of measurement, estimation, and counting. As I listened, I took a couple of pictures of their work and jotted down bits and pieces of their ideas. I wondered: *How can I bring these ideas to the group for consideration? What other tools could I add to the water table to encourage this exploration? How can I give students opportunities to build on these ideas in other parts of our classroom?*

The Feel of the Classroom

ook! Dinosaurs are out today! I'm going to make a house for them!"
Brendan rushed into the classroom, quickly placed his belongings
in his cubby, and made his way to the prehistoric playscape I had
created in the sand bin using plastic dinosaurs, sticks, and rocks.

"Oh, how perfect for you! I'll bet you'll have fun there playing all day. I wish I could play there instead of going to work!" his mom teased in reply.

"I'm going to make a big house for the Apatosaurus, a really small one for the Microraptor, and a super strong one for the T-Rex!" Brendan announced.

"You know your dinosaurs! Sounds like you are going to have a lot of fun today. Ask Mrs. McLennan to send me a picture later of what you build so I can check it out when I'm at work!"

Overhearing their conversation, I walked over to greet Brendan and his mother. "Hi, Brendan! I see you already noticed the dinosaur playscape. I had you in mind when I was searching for materials to place there. I wonder what you'll play today."

As Brendan settled in to explore, his mom gave him a quick kiss and said goodbye. Brendan watched her leave and looked at me. "You'll take a picture of me with the dinosaurs and send it to my mom?" he asked.

"Absolutely! You just tell me when you're ready!" I held up my tablet in reassurance.

BRENDAN WAS in my kindergarten class a few years ago. Because he was a sibling of a child I had previously taught, he and his family were familiar with our classroom and our kindergarten program. And yet, although I had known Brendan since he was two, he experienced severe separation anxiety when it came time to start kindergarten. At the beginning of the year, he found it almost impossible to separate from his mother—kicking, screaming, and crying as she attempted to drop him off and leave the classroom. Brendan would then spend the next hour of school sobbing in his cubby before finally resigning himself to the day at school.

Brendan probably feels like a familiar student to many early childhood teachers. We know that some children seem to transition more easily than others into the school environment. And while differences in individual children certainly exist, it is important that we, as teachers, also consider the factors we control with respect to creating a welcoming and inclusive environment for all of our students.

So, how did Brendan get to the point where he would calmly say goodbye to his mother and enter our classroom eager to engage with new and familiar materials? I believe that several factors related to classroom culture and environment—the feel of the classroom—supported Brendan's transition to kindergarten. Here are the most important ones:

◆ Predictable routines and schedule throughout the day and week

◆ Opportunities to make choices within the structure of the day

◆ Learning materials that reflected his interests and his family and community experiences

◆ A classroom in which his family felt welcome, with multiple ways for families and teachers to engage with one another

With patience and practice, Brendan slowly became comfortable in our space. Although some days he missed his mother more than others, he felt in control of his environment and learning, knowing that his day would be shared with his family. Especially in a time when educators feel pressure to "cover" content and address many standards, it is easy to ask, "What does all of this have to do with math learning?" The type of learning environment we create shapes the mathematical learning that happens within the walls of the classroom and beyond. Children who feel secure and supported are more likely to take risks in their math explorations (Boaler 2016). They persevere through difficult problems and come to view mistakes as opportunities for learning and revising their thinking. They learn that the classroom is a place to ask their own questions and work collaboratively with their peers.

One of the best and simplest ways to begin considering how the classroom environment can support students as thinkers and as people is by asking the children for their opinions. Here are some questions I have found useful when talking with children:

◆ What do you like about our classroom?

◆ What would you change about our classroom?

◆ What spaces in our classroom make you feel good?

- ◆ What spaces in our classroom don't make you feel good?
- ◆ Where do you go when you want to work or play alone?
- ◆ Where do you go when you want to work or play with others?
- ◆ What do you wish we had more of?
- ◆ What do you wish we had less of?

Engaging Families in Math Learning: Stay and Play Days

V era and her son Miles sat together at a table playing an estimation game (see Figure 2.24). Vera was visiting the classroom for the morning on one of our Stay and Play days. The mother and son took turns examining small jars filled with spring trinkets, including small wooden eggs, colorful butterflies, plastic ants, and toy birds. The activity encouraged participants to first estimate how many objects were in the jars before using a math tool like a number grid or ten frame to calculate the actual number of objects. Miles held up the jar of ants and giggled.

love this idea!

FIGURE 2.24
A collection of spring-inspired guessing jars is placed on the table as a math invitation for a Stay and Play family day.

"How many do you think are in there?" his mom asked.

"They are so small! A million!" Miles laughed.

"Now, I don't think a million ants, even if they are teeny-tiny, would fit in there. What's your real guess?" his mom prompted.

"Okay, maybe twenty." Miles poured the ants into his hand. His mom placed a number chart in front of him. He counted by ones as he placed them on the chart one by one. "One, two, three, . . ." Miles counted all the way to twenty-four.

"Twenty-four!" his mom smiled. "That's really close to your estimate!"

Later that morning Vera stood with a cup of coffee in her hands and watched Miles building on the carpet with large wooden blocks. I approached her to chat. "It's amazing to see what he can build," she shared. "At his age, I don't think I would have known to build symmetrical structures. His creations are so beautiful—the detail he puts into them is amazing. When I was younger, I wouldn't have taken risks the way he does. We didn't learn math like you do now. Math used to scare me."

"That's a pretty common feeling," I acknowledged. "I hear that from many parents."

"But I'm glad we can come into the classroom," Vera said, smiling. "It's like I can have a second chance to learn math!"

VERA'S EXPERIENCE was not uncommon. In the many years I have taught kindergarten, I have had the honor of getting to know many families and learning their stories of math fear, embarrassment, interest, or success. It is my hope that by engaging families and the local community in exploring math through play, I can help them reconnect with math learning and perhaps overcome some of their previous negative experiences. As an educator I know that caregivers often default to thinking about school and subjects the way they did as children. If a person did not enjoy math as a child, they sometimes project their feelings of inadequacy, fear, and failure onto their children. Over the years I have heard comments such as these:

FIGURE 2.25

Opening the doors of the classroom and inviting family members to engage in playful math activities with children is a great way to strengthen partnerships, create open communication, and nurture an interest in math.

"I wasn't very good at math. I'm not sure how I'm going to help my kids with their homework when they get older."

"Her dad isn't good with math, so I'm not surprised that she isn't. It must be hereditary."

"Don't send math games home. Math isn't fun. That isn't how we want to spend our time."

It is important to recognize families' feelings about math as valid and to encourage caregivers to share their thoughts and questions. To provide this kind of validation and encouragement, it helps to create an environment that welcomes parents, supports them in sharing the classroom learning, provides information from children's daily experiences at school, and encourages families to continue with their own math learning.

In our classroom, we schedule Stay and Play days throughout the year at different times of day (including the evening) with the hope that all families will be able to attend at some point. Families, caretakers, and other guests participate in daily routines alongside the children and observe the learning that happens during teacher-directed and child-initiated exploration. During Stay and Play days, families explore the classroom and have a chance to review displays of documentation and artifacts of learning (posted paintings, writing, sculptures). Families can also socialize with one another and make connections that might not otherwise grow outside of the classroom. And, of course, the most important part of Stay and Play days are the opportunities for children and their families to play together and talk about mathematics in ways that are open, low risk, and joyful.

Just-Right Conditions for Mathematical Possibility

OUR CLASSROOMS can be welcoming environments that celebrate and inspire children through mathematics. We can create a physical and emotional space that encourages mathematical play and collaboration among students. We can include families in our math learning, while also recognizing the mathematical understanding that they bring with them to the classroom space. By both following the lead of our young learners and keeping in mind the mathematical understandings that are critical to the early childhood years, we can build on children's curiosity and embed authentic moments of math learning throughout our days together.

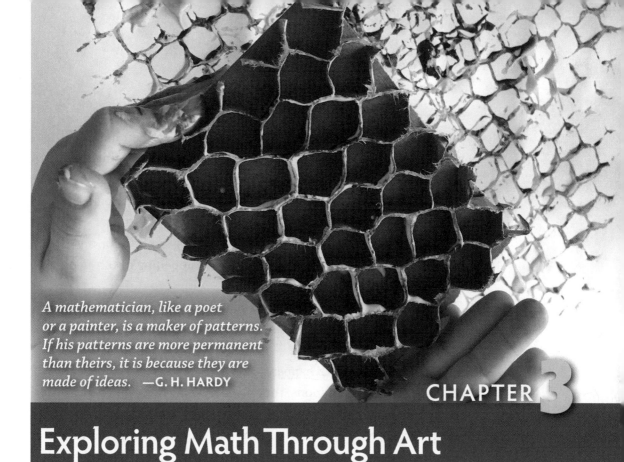

A mathematician, like a poet or a painter, is a maker of patterns. If his patterns are more permanent than theirs, it is because they are made of ideas. —G. H. HARDY

Exploring Math Through Art

FIGURE 3.1
A child uses the hexagonal design on a piece of repurposed cardboard to explore shapes and patterns through art.

O ne afternoon in October several children who had gathered in the art center during choice time noticed a large piece of cardboard. It was thick and shiny and originally meant to provide insulation for a shipment of cold food items. When they took it apart, the children noticed that the internal cardboard piece was shaped like a honeycomb. They hypothesized why this might be:

"Maybe the company thought it would make the box pretty if the cardboard looked like this."

"I think that it's a fancy company, so they want their boxes to be fancy too."

"It reminds me of a beehive . . . Maybe they use honey in their food?"

As they continued to dissect it, the children generated ideas about the function of the cardboard. They were fascinated with peeling off the outer layers of foil and revealing the intricately woven interior. As they explored, I watched from a short distance away. I was curious to see what other theories the children might offer about the cardboard's design and wondered how they planned to use the materials in their artistic creations. I wasn't sure what direction their inquiries might take, so for the moment, I observed quietly—watching the children take apart the cardboard, jotting down a couple of notes on what they were saying, and brainstorming possible ways their wonderings might connect with our math learning.

"This is so pretty. I want to make something out of it for my mom."

"It's like a pattern. The little shapes are happening over and over and over again."

"I don't know . . . Isn't a pattern supposed to be in a straight line?"

"I'm not sure . . . It only uses the same shape. Don't patterns have to use lots of different shapes?"

There it was! As often happens when children are given time and space for playful explorations, they made a connection—in this case to math ideas we had investigated previously in our classroom. We had recently explored and created patterns using a variety of materials and repeatedly returned to the question, "What is a pattern?" Now the children were extending this question in their play. Curious to delve into this idea further, I moved closer to the group and entered the conversation.

"I'm so interested in your thinking. I was listening to your questions about whether or not the cardboard is a pattern. I'm curious about that too. How might you find out? What will you do with the cardboard?"

The children continued to peel and cut the cardboard, murmuring a few ideas without agreeing on a plan of action. I prompted them by referring to a previous time they were unsure of something.

"This reminds me of another time we didn't have enough information." I said. Remember when we weren't sure what kind of insect we found in the grass, and we couldn't find a picture of it in any of our books? What did we do?"

"Oh! I know!" said Leah. "We asked someone else! We tweeted a picture of it, and someone else knew and answered us!"

"That's right," I responded. "We asked other people for their opinions and ideas and used them to help us come up with our own ideas. I wonder if we can do something similar with this piece of cardboard."

Leah's face lit up with a connection. "I know! Let's ask everyone in our class what they think! We can make it our Question of the Day. I'll go write the question now!"

As Leah headed off to write her question on the communal easel located by the classroom door, the remaining children at the center decided the cardboard would make interesting paint prints. They spent the rest of the choice time brushing pieces of cardboard with different colors of paint and then stamping them on large pieces of paper, creating their own patterned designs (see Figure 3.1). Later that day, in a whole-group discussion, the children shared artwork created using the cardboard and explored Leah's question. Together they debated whether the cardboard honeycomb and the painted prints they created with it were patterns.

Leah was the first to offer an idea. "I think it's a pattern because it has shapes in it. Patterns always have shapes."

"No, that can't be right," disagreed Julius. "Patterns use lots of different things. My brother had a pattern with numbers in his homework last night. My mom helped him."

"I don't think it's a pattern at all. It's all over the place. Patterns should be in a line so you can see them. I can't tell what the pattern is so it's not a pattern" added Aaron.

"It *is* a pattern. It's like the little squares on my shirt. See! Look! A pattern that is all over, just like the cardboard! A pattern is something happening again and again," exclaimed Mia, pointing excitedly at her shirt to emphasize the point.

I remained quiet during the children's debate, listening to the ideas inspired by the cardboard art. I wasn't concerned about arriving at a conclusion on this day regarding whether the cardboard was a pattern. What was important was the deep thinking about patterns I was observing and allowing children the time and space to question and debate their ideas. As the conversation wrapped up for the day, I considered what pattern provocation I might set out the next day so we could continue to explore these ideas together.

Artful Math and Mathful Art:
The Power of Playing with Math and Art Together

CHILDREN ARE natural artists. Anyone who has ever watched a young child draw or paint for the first time knows that children do not require formal lessons or guidance in order to begin to make art. When given opportunities to explore, children come up with creative ideas, ask and investigate their own questions, and develop a sense of self and community through their art. And the same can be said of their relationship to math! Children are capable mathematicians with their own ideas and ways of problem solving long before they enter school. Integrating the study of math and art allows children to continue to build confidence in their own ideas as well as to work collaboratively and creatively to explore new ideas.

FIGURE 3.2
A child explores shapes by sculpting with clay using a variety of tools.

In this chapter, we will consider several ways that art and math can be interwoven meaningfully in the classroom. We will

- ◆ explore how an art center can give children the time and space to **engage with open explorations that highlight mathematical ideas**;

- ◆ consider how teachers can invite students to **engage in art around specific math ideas**;

- ◆ focus on how **studying artists as mentors can inspire both mathematical thinking and artistic creativity**; and

- ◆ reflect on ways that teachers and students can **appreciate art and math beyond the walls of the classroom**.

Creating a Space of Mathematical Possibility: Open Exploration in the Art Center

One December our class began to explore movement and pathways at the building center. Using repurposed boards and blocks, children constructed various ramps, hypothesizing how fast and far a rolling object might travel after being launched downward. Through their play, students discovered that the steeper the slope of the ramp was, the faster and farther an object would roll.

Curious to see how they would engage with this interest and understanding in another context, I offered large cardboard boxes, trays, and tubes, as well as marbles, tennis balls, and paper in our art area. I placed a large tablecloth underneath the workspace to catch any dripping paint.

The children immediately noticed the art invitation and set to work. They began by creating a connected system of ramps using the boxes and tubes. Then they experimented with how the balls and marbles rolled down the tubes, placing cardboard trays at the bottom to catch the balls. Once satisfied with their ramp creations, the students placed paper in the trays. Dipping balls and marbles in paint,

FIGURE 3.3
A child creates his own clay spheres for exploration with ramps and paint.

they rolled them down the ramps. Students delighted at the lengths of painted tracks that were created on the paper by the rolling objects as they exited the tubes. During choice time over the next several weeks, they continued to sculpt spheres using a variety of materials, including clay, and used these items in place of the balls, comparing whether these materials behaved similarly when rolled down the ramps (see Figure 3.3).

Listening to students' conversations allowed me to notice connections they made between their experiences building with ramps and this new art experience. I noticed that in the art center the painted lines became a record of the distance the balls traveled. The children were curious to see who could create the longest painted track, and the experience soon turned into a measurement activity. The students experimented with ways of measuring and recording each person's track, with some students devoting the entire choice time to this activity. Although art making was not the focus of the children's conversations, at the end of their time in the art center, they began to notice the beauty in the intersecting colors and lines created by the various trials of balls and marbles rolling in paint.

TEACHER TIP

Consider setting up an iPad or other video recording device to record a time-lapse video of children's explorations in the art center. Video can be a helpful tool for children to reflect on their work and generate new questions to explore. These videos can also be shared with families as a form of documentation or posted on a class blog. Some children may want to do some writing to accompany the video, providing instructions or questions for those blog visitors who might also wish to replicate the activity at home or in their own classrooms.

DURING THE NEXT outdoor time, some children asked if they could take the materials outside for further exploration. They hoped to continue their quest to see who could roll their ball the farthest. By leaning the tubes against the low-hanging branches of our pine tree, the children were able to create various angles with the ramps.

While specific art- and math-content ideas emerged through this exploration in the art center, perhaps the greatest thing the children gained from this experience was the freedom of time and space to engage in the work of mathematicians and artists. As they designed systems of ramps and rolled paint-covered balls down the ramps to create art, the children learned how to

- ask and investigate self-directed questions ("Which ball will go the farthest?" "How will moving the ramp change how far the ball rolls?");

- reason about how and why something might or might not work ("I think making the ramp really steep will make the ball go really fast so that it goes really far." "If my ball has too much paint on it, it will get stuck.");

- revise their ideas ("When I made the ramp too steep, the ball just fell off, so I'm moving the ramp so it's not quite so steep." "I'm putting less paint on my ball this time.");

- work collaboratively ("If you hold the ramp higher, I can roll the ball at the same time." "Can you help me attach the ramps together? I can't do it by myself.");

◆ use tools purposefully ("I can use duct tape to hold those pieces together." "Maybe a smaller brush will put less paint on the ball."); and

◆ record ideas for further reflection ("I want to take a picture of what we've created so next time I know how to set it up again." "I'm going to draw a picture of this so I can show my dad what we did.").

In the Reggio Emilia approach to early childhood education, children are encouraged to use their curiosity and questions about the world as provocations for their inquiries and projects. Reggio Emilia–inspired educators often refer to the "hundred languages" children use to explore and represent their emerging theories about the world (Edwards, Gandini, and Forman 1998). Whether or not we work in Reggio Emilia–inspired programs, the classroom art center allows for a natural and powerful merging of art and math as children work in different mediums to express their understanding of the world around them.

FIGURE 3.4
A vase of flowers and saucers of paint on the art table invite children to explore color mixing and still life painting.

Setting Up the Art Center

Maddie and Eve work side by side at a table in the art center. In front of them is a collection of jars and brushes. A variety of colors of paint are available in terra-cotta saucers, and the girls are using spoons to dole out various amounts into small empty jars. They are working together to mix a new shade that is needed for a painting of a vase of flowers. Maddie and Eve are hoping to paint a still life, but the exact colors they want are not currently available. I have intentionally not provided these colors in order to encourage the children to problem solve, using measurement and proportional reasoning while working with the paint.

"That's not it," Maddie exclaims as she holds a saturated paintbrush next to the vase of flowers on the table, seeing whether the color matches the pale-yellow rose. "See, the rose is lighter. We need to add more white."

"But I've already added four spoons of the white to the jar. If I add more it might be too light," responds Eve.

"What if you only add two more spoonfuls this time. Or we can add them one by one. If you add too much white, then we'll just add more yellow to balance it," suggests Maddie.

The girls continue to add small spoonfuls of white and yellow to their jar, testing and retesting until they are satisfied that the shade of yellow they have created matches the rose.

OUR ART CENTER, where Maddie and Eve painted that day, is located in the corner of our classroom, framed by large windows from which children can peer out onto the playground. The view from the window, where children can notice the changing seasons and animal visitors, often inspires their creations. Art, however, can happen anywhere, at any time. You do not need a fancy classroom space to engage children in mathematically inspired art. In fact, while having a dedicated art center where you can keep ongoing projects and store materials is ideal, making an art center can be as simple as clearing off a table during choice time and gathering some materials for children to explore. What matters most is having an inviting area where children have basic materials, time, and freedom to explore and create on a regular basis.

Whether you are setting up an art center for the first time or building on what you already have in place, consider these ways in which you might provide space and materials that invite open exploration:

◆ **Build the art space with the children.** At the beginning of the year, our art center consists of a table, a child-sized easel, a light table, wall space for display, a drying rack, and some empty shelves. I introduce new materials, tools, and techniques to students over time, and then they become part of our art center. This slow introduction helps children feel confident and independent when visiting the art center.

FIGURE 3.5
Different shades and tints of paint can be mixed by children and stored in repurposed jars for future use.

FIGURE 3.6
Blue and green objects are first sorted by children and then stored together on an art shelf.

FIGURE 3.7
Ribbon is ordered by color and can be stored on a paper towel dispenser for easy access.

◆ **Provide a table with chairs so that children can work together on a communal project or engage with one another's work while sitting side by side or across from each other.** Having an open, available space encourages children to engage in discussions as they work, providing opportunities for rich oral language exchanges that can include math talk.

◆ **Consider creating an art shelf near the art center.** Placing a shelf at the perimeter of the art center can define the area and create a cozy space away from busier parts of the room. Additionally, the shelf provides easy access to purchased, found, and repurposed art materials from which children can choose.

◆ **Inspire students with materials.** Place interesting objects on the table to provoke exploration and conversation (e.g., a basket of shells and pastels, translucent paper and markers, tinted water and droppers, colorful paper in various sizes). Continually rotate these materials so that there is always something new to explore in the

FIGURE 3.8
A light table enhances artistic exploration of line and shape when children explore materials such as paint and shaving cream on its surface.

art center. If you do not have a dedicated art table, these materials can be stored on a shelf and brought out during choice time. For a list of possible materials to include in your art center, see the textbox "Materials to Inspire Children's Art."

◆ **Organize materials.** Available art materials can be sorted and displayed by type of material, color, texture, and size in clear jars and containers. This display of materials highlights a purpose for classifying and sorting, and it also helps children find materials and return them to their proper location after use. The teacher should not do this organizing work alone; children love to help with the task of organizing materials! I often notice children engaging in mathematical thinking as they organize the available materials. Children might work together to decide how to sort a large donated collection of feathers by color, size, or texture. If they want to empty a bag of beads into a container for easier access, they may discuss which size container will hold all of the beads.

◆ **Display children's artwork.** When we display children's work in the classroom, we send the message that we value their ideas and processes. Consider displaying children's art in frames around the room and creating binders of art in laminated page protectors that children and families can browse. You may even consider laminating some of the children's art (thus making it waterproof) to hang outside on a fence or other permanent structure to beautify and inspire outdoor play.

MATERIALS TO INSPIRE CHILDREN'S ART

While creating an art center can be as simple as putting out some paper and paint, having the opportunity to explore with a variety of materials can be engaging and productive for young artists.

Over the years, these are some materials I have found to inspire children's art making.

Art-Making Tools

- Scissors and paper cutters
- Stapler
- Tape (clear, masking, packing)
- Glue (bottles, sticks, pens, guns)
- Paintbrushes (various sizes of brush and lengths of handle)
- Hole punches
- Clay cutters
- Spray bottles
- Squeeze bottles
- Palettes
- Plastic cups
- Rulers
- Protractors
- Geometric compasses
- Paint rollers
- Dough rollers
- Tweezers
- Pipettes
- Magnifying glasses
- Baking trays
- Sponges
- Muffin tins

Mark-Making Materials

- Pencils
- Erasers
- Colored pencils
- Sharpeners
- Crayons
- Pastels
- Paints (watercolors, acrylics, finger paint)
- Chalk
- Sidewalk chalk
- Pens
- Markers
- Modeling dough
- Clay
- Dry erase markers

Natural Materials

- Pine cones
- Sticks
- Shells
- Pebbles
- Feathers
- Leaves
- Acorns
- Fresh and dried flowers
- Seeds
- Dried corn and beans
- Pine needles

Consumable and Repurposed Materials

- A variety of sizes, colors, and thicknesses of paper (sketch paper, construction paper, finger-painting paper, grid paper)
- Cardboard
- Ribbon
- Pom-poms
- Rubber bands
- Stickers
- Pipe cleaners
- Bottle caps and lids
- Repurposed jars
- Yogurt cups
- Greeting card fronts
- Wood scraps
- Metal odds and ends (e.g., repurposed keys, nuts and bolts)

- Plastic tubing
- Large-appliance boxes
- Egg cartons
- Repurposed magazines
- Fabric swatches
- Broken costume jewelry
- Odd puzzle pieces
- Beads
- Corks
- Bubble wrap
- Packing peanuts
- Buttons
- Yarn
- Felt

- Sponge
- Straws
- Cotton balls
- Clothespins
- Bubble wrap
- Wooden sticks and dowels
- Wallpaper scraps

FIGURE 3.9
A child explores shapes and patterns while making prints with bubble wrap.

Repurposed Tools

- Kitchen utensils (mashers, presses, rollers) can be wonderful sculpting tools for clay and modeling dough or be used to stamp paint.
- Miniature decorative spoons and forks can be useful for spooning, measuring, and mixing different consumable materials.
- Metal nesting bowls can be used as an inviting way to present materials in the center of an art-making space.
- Muffin tins or ice cube trays are effective tools for helping children sort and display materials for easy use (e.g., sorting pom-poms by color). They can also be used as paint palettes for color mixing: the primary colors can be offered in three sections of the tray, and children can create their own shades in the empty spaces.
- Paper towel dispensers can hold spools of ribbon or paper.
- Lazy Susan spinning organizers can be placed in the middle of a table to provide easy access to a variety of materials.

FIGURE 3.10
Children create circular designs by stamping paint with plungers during outdoor play.

FIGURE 3.11
Clothing hangers can be repurposed as child-friendly "easels" that can hang on many outdoor surfaces.

TEACHER TIP

The art center can transcend the classroom walls. Bringing very messy activities outdoors allows for a more freeing experience, for both students and their teachers, who won't have to worry as much about splattered paint and sticky floors! Art materials can easily be stored in baskets and transported outside using a cart or wagon. Fences can serve as easels, and papers can easily be clipped and hung using either clothespins or repurposed children's clothing hangers. Art can be left outside to dry until the end of the school day.

Noticing and Naming the Math Learning

O ne winter day the children noticed a telephone wire just outside of our schoolyard. Freezing rain had caused it to sag, and our custodian had placed cones near the fence in order to discourage children from getting too close to the wire. The children were full of questions, wondering what the wire was for and how it would be fixed. That afternoon I invited the students to create sculptures in the art center by gluing various colors and lengths of paper strips onto a cardboard base (see Figure 3.12). The paper sculptures reminded me of the sagging telephone wire outside, and I wondered if the children would make this connection, too, as they explored the materials.

As I observed the children manipulating the strips, I was interested in seeing how they worked with the materials, what connections they might make to their own lives and experiences, and whether there were opportunities for me to highlight math ideas in our discussions. I sat down next to a few children in the art center and explored the materials alongside them, modeling how the paper could be folded, twisted, and affixed to the base by gluing both ends. Some children watched and replicated my techniques as they worked; others explored their own ideas independently.

"What are you doing?" Charlie directed his question at me.

I used his question as an opportunity for a minilesson and inserted some new language into my directions.

"I'm trying to manipulate the paper. I'm changing it in

FIGURE 3.12
Children create paper sculptures by manipulating paper strips and attaching them to a cardboard base using glue.

different ways. Watch. I can fold it in opposite directions to make it look like zigzags, or I can curve or spiral it. If I glue the ends down, then the paper will stay the way I have created it. I can even place my strips over and under each other."

Charlie nodded his head and spent the next several minutes creating with his paper strips, incorporating many of my strategies into his work. As I watched, I decided to ask him to present his artwork during our sharing circle at the end of choice time. This would give Charlie and me the opportunity to share the same ideas and vocabulary with the entire group of children, especially important for those who had not visited the art center that day. Perhaps during outdoor play, children would notice the hanging wire again, and I could reference our paper sculpting. I could point out how it was difficult to affix heavy paper to the base, helping children build their theories about why the wire was still hanging so low.

CHILDREN ARE curious and inventive and often eager to engage with one another in collaborative and exploratory activities while visiting the art center. Although materials and tools are often modeled during whole-group instruction, children are encouraged to freely explore and create in personalized ways. When visiting the art center, I am able to observe, question, extend, experiment with, and reflect upon the entire artistic process with children. Engaging in conversation while children are creating provides opportunities for me to notice and name aloud the math learning I am observing, surfacing ideas for us to explore further together. Consider the previous vignette. When the children were interested in gluing long strips of paper to a base in different ways (loops, arches, zigzag lines), they created complex paper sculptures. After observing their work, I was able to express an interest in and describe my thoughts about the pattern and measurement ideas I noticed. Taking the lead from the students, we explored questions like "What happens when you fold the paper in half?" "What happens to the length of the strips when you fold them like an accordion?" and "What new patterns can I create in my sculpture by folding, twisting, and looping paper?"

FIGURE 3.13
A child organizes repurposed paint chips by sorting them into groups by color.

Here are some open-ended explorations I have found particularly productive for young children's mathematical thinking. As you think about which ones you might try out, consider what mathematical ideas might come out of children's work. How will you highlight and build upon their ideas through noticing and wondering alongside your students?

PAPER SCULPTURES

Suggested Materials: long strips of colorful construction paper cut into various widths, a large piece of cardboard for the base, glue sticks, scissors

What's the Math? Describe measurable attributes of objects; directly compare two objects with a measurable attribute in common; describe objects in the environment using names of shapes; and describe the relative positions of these objects.

Teacher Tips: Provide the strips of paper in a large basket in the middle of your working area. Invite interested children to choose a large piece of cardboard to serve as a base for their sculpture. Encourage children to mentally plan and talk about what types of lines they might like to include in their paper structure (e.g., straight, curved, zigzag, twisted). Model

how one end of the paper can be glued to the cardboard base. Carefully manipulate the paper strip. If you are twisting it, for example, show how one hand can hold down the glued end to keep it from lifting off the cardboard while the other hand can gently twist the strip. Once you are satisfied with the appearance of the strip, glue the other end to the cardboard base (see Figure 3.12). As children work, encourage them to discuss the shapes and lines they see emerging in their work, the length of the paper strips they are using, and the location of the strips in relation to one another. For instance, you might say, "I see that you needed to place the zigzag strip under the curved strip to get it to stick to the cardboard base and not fall off." Children can also work on one large, collaborative paper sculpture that can be displayed in the classroom.

TEXTURED PRINTS

Suggested Materials: repurposed materials, including textured fabric swatches and bubble wrap, paint, rubber bands, paper, rolling pins, brushes

What's the Math? Describe and name shapes regardless of their orientation or overall size; identify and describe patterns.

Teacher Tips: Demonstrate to children that the repurposed materials (e.g., fabrics with different textures, bubble wrap) can be attached to a rolling pin with rubber bands so the material covers much of the pin's surface. Lightly brush the covered pin with paint. Encourage the children to roll the pin over their paper and observe the interesting shapes and patterns that emerge in the prints. Repeat with different materials covering the rolling pins. As children notice the patterns and designs emerge, engage them in a discussion about what they are noticing and wondering.

FIGURE 3.14
A child creates prints by first wrapping a rolling pin with rubber bands and then covering it in paint.

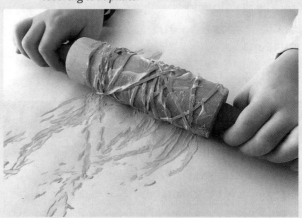

TAPE RESIST PAINTING

Suggested Materials: heavy paper (e.g., card stock, cardboard), painter's tape, paint, thick brushes

What's the Math? Describe and name shapes regardless of their orientation or overall size; describe measurable attributes of objects; directly compare two objects with a measurable attribute in common.

Teacher Tips: Encourage children to place tape on the paper in different ways (shapes, lines, patterns). Invite children to paint all over the paper, covering as much of the area as they can. While the paint is still wet, gently peel the tape off the paper, revealing the unpainted designs underneath. Encourage children to discuss their creations, paying careful attention to the surprising lines and shapes that are revealed and using math language to describe what they see. Children can compare the results of their tape paintings with one another or share them with the class during a sharing circle, inviting observation and feedback from their peers.

FROZEN CREATIONS

Suggested Materials: various sizes and shapes of containers (e.g., repurposed plastic tubs, muffin tins, small cake pans), water in a large tub, a variety of natural loose parts (e.g., acorns, seeds, dried corn or beans), measuring cups and spoons, freezer space

What's the Math? Estimate and count; describe and name shapes regardless of their orientation or overall size; describe measurable attributes of objects; build an early understanding of capacity, time, and temperature.

Teacher Tips: Although this activity can happen any place and time, doing it in colder climates will extend its duration. Children select a container and estimate, then count, how many cups or spoonfuls of water it takes to fill. Encourage children to select, count, and place a variety of loose parts into the water. Listen to students' ideas and make your own noticings and wonderings about how the materials are responding to the water, For example, you might say, "I am noticing most of the pebbles are sinking and filling the bottom of your container" or "You filled the entire container with ten large and five small pine cones" or "I wonder how much water has spilled over the top of your tray as you've added more and more seeds." Place the containers in a freezer or outside on a cold day. When the creations are frozen, pop them out of the containers and place them in different locations in your play area or outside your classroom windows. Encourage children to make predictions about how quickly the ice will melt, and record observations over time. Ask students how they might measure the ice melt. Possible suggestions include measuring the size of the ice block over time or measuring the water as the ice melts.

FIGURE 3.15
A child holds a piece of ice formed into a heart.

SPLATTER PAINTING

Suggested Materials: small plastic bins, large rubber bands, paint, brushes, thick card stock, scissors, goggles

What's the Math? Describe measurable attributes of objects; directly compare two objects with a measurable attribute in common.

Teacher Tips: Explain to children that they are going to use the rubber bands to splatter paint. (Goggles are recommended so that splattered paint does not end up in children's eyes.) Children should first select a paper that is the correct size to fit inside their bin or cut the paper to the right size. Next, the bin must be fitted with rubber bands that wrap around the opened side. Once five or six rubber bands are in place, the children can gently brush each rubber band with a light coat of paint. When the rubber bands are coated, the children can gently pluck and snap them, causing the paint to splatter and leave interesting speckled designs on the paper. Encourage the children to apply various levels of force to the rubber band and observe what happens. What kind of splatter does a rubber band pulled lightly produce? What about rubber bands plucked more forcefully? Does the length or width of the rubber band have an impact on what type of art is produced? Do the colors of paint mix on the paper into new shades? Encourage children to discuss their predictions, observations, and explorations as they manipulate the materials. Change the size of the bin and see what effect this has on the art produced.

FIGURE 3.16
A child plucks rubber bands covered with paint to create splatter designs on the paper.

Building on Children's Explorations with Teacher Invitations

ONE WAY to build on ideas that emerge through children's play is to highlight them in class meetings and invite other children to explore the ideas discovered by their classmates. At times, I purposely design an ongoing art project that extends specific math ideas. For example,

FIGURE 3.17
Children can explore the colors, lines, and patterns on repurposed fabric swatches.

when I planned for children to explore patterns in the world around them, I offered a basket of interesting fabric swatches on the art table (see Figure 3.17). Children used these fabric pieces in their own artwork, incorporating and extending the color, shape, and texture patterns they noticed. In the sections below, you will read about two ongoing projects involving symmetry and shape. However, you might develop an art project about any math content that is important to your curriculum and inspiring to your students.

Investigating Symmetry

After painting at the easel, Noah removed a large paper, folded it in half, and placed it in the rack to dry. His friend José immediately noticed and pointed out his error.

"If you leave it folded in the drying rack, it will dry stuck together and you won't be able to open it."

Heeding José's advice, Noah removed his painting and carefully opened it. He gasped upon viewing his art—what had been a painting of his mom had transformed into a symmetrical smattering of mixed colors.

"It's not my mom anymore!" exclaimed Noah. "Look! This side looks the same as this side!" By folding and unfolding the painting while it was wet, Noah had inadvertently created a new, symmetrical piece of artwork. Interested in further testing their ideas about folding paper, Noah and José spent the rest of their time at the art center, dabbing paint onto paper, folding it, and opening it to reveal symmetrical creations filled with interesting colors and designs.

FREEDOM TO EXPERIMENT while engaging in art making often leads to surprising results. When children are encouraged to mess about and engage fully with the materials, they notice how their work changes when the same objects are manipulated in different ways. A painting becomes very different if it is folded and pressed together while wet. Children delight in the new forms their artwork takes when they open the paper, noticing how the colors blend and spread together, creating new designs. As they do this, they are experiencing symmetry firsthand, recognizing that when the paper is folded in the middle, each half becomes a mirror reflection of the other.

SYMMETRY IN A BUTTERFLY INVESTIGATION

Symmetry is a topic that intrigues artists, mathematicians, and nature lovers alike. It can be observed in flowers, butterflies, birds, fruit, leaves, snowflakes, shells, and even the human face. Often ideas about symmetry naturally emerge in the art center, as demonstrated by José and Noah's work with folding painted papers.

Around the same time that José and Noah were exploring symmetry through painting, some children in the class became interested in the butterflies they noticed landing on the weeds around the perimeter of our schoolyard.

"I can't believe such beautiful butterflies would like these weeds!" Carter laughed one day at recess.

"Butterflies need to eat just like us! They don't care if the flowers are weeds." Samantha replied.

The children watched the butterflies over several days, drawing their observations in sketch notebooks (see Figure 3.19). I pointed out the visible symmetry on their wings and encouraged them to replicate it in their colorful drawings. Some children went on to wonder *why* the patterns on the butterflies' wings were symmetrical, and spent time finding and reading books about butterflies from the school library. The children refined and researched their questions about butterfly symmetry with my help: "What is the purpose of their symmetrical designs?" "What colors and patterns are seen on the butterfly species in our area?" "What different sizes and body shapes do butterflies have?" "What other animals in our neighborhood have symmetrical patterns on their bodies?"

Using the information they discovered, the children then set about creating their own interpretations and representations of what butterflies are to them, incorporating symmetry into their designs.

FIGURE 3.19
A child's drawing of a symmetrical butterfly observed in the schoolyard.

Some children carefully drew an outline with marker on pieces of repurposed plastic and then painted over the plastic with acrylics to showcase the design and symmetry in the butterflies they observed. The butterflies were then cut out and affixed to a branch for display, fluttering in the air as small breezes passed by. Other children chose to sculpt butterflies out of clay. They carved intricate details on the wings and then painted over the designs once they dried. Still other children created butterflies using loose parts, including broken pottery and sea glass (see Figure 3.20). These butterflies were placed around the classroom to decorate and inspire, reminding us of the intersection of our artistic, mathematical, and scientific investigations.

SYMMETRY IN SELF-PORTRAITS

Each year our class also spends time exploring the symmetry in our faces while drawing or painting self-portraits multiple times across the school year (in the fall, winter, and spring). Children first examine themselves in mirrors set up on tables. I encourage them to spend time playing with their reflection before drawing. They make faces and notice the nuances of how their features move and change, and how the symmetry is fluid, adapting as their faces change with emotion and expression. When they are comfortable, they use pencils to sketch on canvas the outline of what they see, paying particular attention to the details of their features and ensuring their representations are balanced. The children quickly realize that, for their portraits to be recognizable when hung on our wall, their facial features need to be drawn to scale and be symmetrically represented. Children offer one another constructive feedback about how to improve the portraits so they are more realistic. As their skills develop and improve over the year, they can compare their previous portraits with the current ones, reflecting upon their work and appreciating the change and growth in their abilities. With time and experience, children begin to point out symmetrical objects around their homes and schools, with those that they consider most interesting usually found outdoors in nature.

SYMMETRY IN TRANSIENT ART

Children in our classroom also explore the concept of symmetry by creating transient artwork in our classroom or schoolyard using a variety of loose parts. We define a space for the art by placing repurposed frames, mirror squares, or mats in a central location—sometimes this is on our art table; other times we bring these materials outdoors. Children are invited to manipulate and arrange loose parts (e.g., repurposed caps, gems, wood cookies, tiles, buttons) or natural materials (e.g., pine cones, pebbles, leaves, sticks) in innovative ways, often incorporating balance and symmetry into their design. Transient art focuses on the process of creation, and when the children are done exploring, they return the materials to storage containers, leaving a fresh space for the next artist to use. Because transient art does not require children to commit to an idea or design, it is often freeing and encourages children to take risks in their artistic explorations. Taking photos can preserve the art for children, and the photos can be added to a digital portfolio or shared during later discussions.

Sometimes we've even created transient art with natural loose parts and left it outdoors for others to discover! On the day of a large open house welcoming potential new students and their families to kindergarten registration, our children created and left large collaborative transient art pieces on the front sidewalk, composed solely of artifacts they had found in our schoolyard. Inspired by the work of natural artist Andy Goldsworthy, they sought to create with only what they could find, and then leave the art outdoors to be appreciated by passersby, knowing that the art would eventually be scattered and disappear. In addition to including symmetry and balance, these large projects required collaboration and communication among children in order to be aesthetically pleasing and successful, embedding rich social problem solving into the experience.

Incorporating Shape

The world around us is composed of shapes, and children often marvel at the unique designs and creations that are recognizable in natural and man-made objects. While some of the shapes they notice might be the two- and three-dimensional shapes we traditionally study in school (i.e., circles, triangles, rectangles, spheres, and cubes), children also notice other, less-defined shapes that we often overlook in school (e.g., leaves, flowers, clouds, hearts).

Shapes of all kinds can be explored through art. Two-dimensional and more organic shapes can be included in painting and drawing, while three-dimensional shapes can be integrated into sculpture and construction. Creating with loose parts that embody shape (e.g., glass beads, plastic pipes, wooden blocks) helps children consider composition from multiple perspectives as they create. Children who are encouraged to build with three-dimensional objects must consider the ways in which the materials interact (Pelo 2007). They can consider the way the shapes fit together or

FIGURE 3.21
A child arranges translucent pattern blocks onto a sheet of clear contact paper placed in a sunny window.

oppose each other as they work on integrating balance and symmetry into their aesthetic designs. This provides opportunity for educators to introduce new vocabulary, materials, and tools as they model their use in playful explorations with children. Looking at examples of how shape is used in the world around us can inspire children's play and work. Here are some activities that spotlight the richness and complexity of shape:

- **Go on a shape walk** in your community and take photos of interesting structures that you see. Print and laminate the photos so children can draw on them and talk with each other about what they notice, perhaps outlining and counting the various shapes they see. These photographs can serve to inspire their artistic creations in the classroom as well.

- **Take a virtual field trip** (e.g., Google Earth, online image search) to another place and explore natural and man-made wonders of the world. Explore these using a mathematical lens to find balance, symmetry, color, and shape. Encourage children to recreate these using wooden blocks or repurposed materials.

- **Challenge children to discover** interesting ways to sort uncommon objects (see Figure 3.22). Ask them to explain what is the same about the grouped objects and to describe the sorting rule used.

- **Incorporate mixed media creations** at the art center and encourage children to add a variety of materials to traditional artwork (e.g., adding foam to paintings, gluing felt pieces to drawings). Ask them to explain how the variety of materials enhances their artwork. Encourage children to share their artwork during a whole-group discussion. Teachers and other children can comment on the math they notice in each piece of art.

- **Build transient or permanent art outdoors** with repurposed materials (e.g., boxes, cans, paper rolls) and natural artifacts (e.g., sticks, rocks, logs). Take photos of the creations and share them with digital pen pals using social media. Print the photos and encourage children to write mathematically about what they created.

For example, the children might describe the steps they took in block construction; the materials they used; and the height, width, and length of their creations. The photos and descriptions can be added to a book about structures and kept in the classroom for future reference.

◆ **Stamp common objects into paint** and make prints on paper in order to observe the shapes that are present in everyday objects. For instance, a tube stamped in paint will leave a circular mark. Encourage families to repurpose these paintings as seasonal gift wrap for sharing with family and friends.

◆ **Encourage problem solving and risk taking** in children's construction activities. Brainstorm questions such as "What kind of base is best when building a tall tower? Why?" "What can you use to make a repeating print? How do you know?"

◆ **Look for shapes and patterns** in everyday objects such as fabric and wallpaper samples. These can be provided at the art center, and children can extend or modify what they see by drawing on paper.

FIGURE 3.22
Loose parts are sorted by color and arranged into a color wheel that is displayed in the art area.

Understanding Artist Mentors Through a Mathematical Lens

One day in the late fall the class was working with loose parts, including various colors and sizes of buttons, gems, and sea glass. Placed in front of each student was a laminated copy of Van Gogh's *Starry Night*. Each child interpreted the artwork in a different way. One child used black buttons to outline the shapes he noticed in the swirls in the sky; another child counted the gems needed to fill the black structure on the left-hand side of the piece; a third child placed yellow gems inside each of the starbursts in the sky, counting how many there were in total.

I first introduced *Starry Night* to the children after they had shared stories with me of noticing the beautiful colors of the sky at dusk in our own area. We had recently experienced daylight saving time, and they were curious about why the sky was darkening earlier, and amazed by the wonderful shades of red, orange, and blue that emerged each night over the Detroit River. I was curious about the (often mathematical) language the children used in their descriptions—the number of colors they saw, the shape and direction of the clouds on the horizon, the contrast between boats on the river and the colors being illuminated in the background—and I wanted to give them something tangible to explore in the classroom. By offering this invitation, I hoped that the children might make a connection between their own night sky and the one represented in Van Gogh's work, mathematizing it in different ways by using loose parts to physically explore the colors, shapes, and lines they noticed. After our work with *Starry Night*, we shared our observations in a math circle. I then offered the children a laminated photo of the Detroit River with a beautiful dusky sky in the background and invited them to explore it in the same way.

BRINGING THE WORK of respected artists into your classroom can inspire children to learn new art processes and techniques, which can then be practiced in your art center. This experience can also

inspire rich conversation as children observe and interpret works of art. Incorporating these pieces can be especially helpful for educators who are "art shy" or feel unsure about using certain artistic techniques or materials themselves. Many artists integrate color, shape, pattern, and proportional reasoning into their pieces, providing a context for mathematical appreciation and discussion with students, and hopefully inspiring children to continue exploring these ideas at the art center and beyond. In our classroom, I offer art books at centers for children to browse, as well as copies of famous works of art. In our whole-class discussions, we sometimes display a piece of art using the Smartboard or overhead projector for children to manipulate and explore. Here are some artists who might inspire the mathematical artists in your classroom:

- ◆ Addye Nieves — shape, color, line
- ◆ Agnes Martin — shape, pattern, line
- ◆ Bridget Riley — line, shape, color
- ◆ Dale Chihuly — color, shape, texture

- Deborah Roberts — shape, proportional reasoning
- Elaine Sturtevant — pattern
- Elizabeth Catlett — pattern, color
- Frida Kahlo — pattern, contrast
- Georges Seurat — pointillism
- Georgia O'Keeffe — shape, pattern, proportional reasoning, color
- Gustav Klimt — pattern
- Helen Frankenthaler — color, shape, pattern
- Henri Matisse — shape
- Judy Chicago — shape
- Kehinde Wiley — color, pattern
- Louise Bourgeois — proportional reasoning
- Pablo Picasso — proportional reasoning
- Piet Mondrian — color, line, shape
- Romare Bearden — shape, line, color, proportional reasoning
- Vincent van Gogh — color, shape, line
- Wassily Kandinsky — line, shape

Art Beyond the Classroom Walls

IN ADDITION to works by respected artists that can be presented in the classroom, there are also many examples of mathematically inspired artwork to appreciate in your local community—geometric designs painted on the sides of barns, tile mosaics found on city fountains, shapes that constitute a building's architecture, sculptures in many gardens, and murals beautifying subway stops. Art can be found everywhere! Consider taking your class on a walking tour of your local city block or school neighborhood, or taking them on a bus to a nearby art gallery or museum. Children can identify and describe the math they notice in the world around them and take digital photos or draw sketches for later classroom observation and discussion. For those classrooms that use Twitter to share information and engage in discussions with others, photos of the math found around the community and beyond can be tweeted along with the hashtag #foundmath. Users from around the world enjoy sharing the everyday math they observe and appreciate in their daily lives using this hashtag. Perusing what others have found by scrolling through a search of the hashtag may provoke interesting discussions among your students and inspire them to look at everyday objects in new ways, even when going on a community walk isn't possible.

Children make sense of the world around them by observing, asking questions, and trying things out. They do not experience the world through separate art and math lenses, although our school structures sometimes encourage this way of thinking. When children are encouraged to engage in process-based art making on a regular basis, they become empowered to go beyond the acquisition of simple, declarative

FIGURE 3.24
Toronto's subway stations are full of public art, including this ceramic tile mosaic, part of the series The Whole Is Greater Than the Sum of Its Parts, *by Rebecca Bayer and David Gregory.*

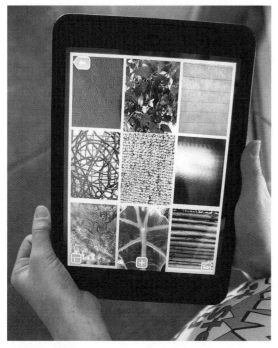

FIGURE 3.25
A child uses a tablet to capture and organize photos of patterns she finds in the world around her.

knowledge and instead explore artistic and mathematical ideas that both enrich and surpass content standards. The ideas in this chapter are just a starting point. The possibilities are as endless and creative as art and math themselves.

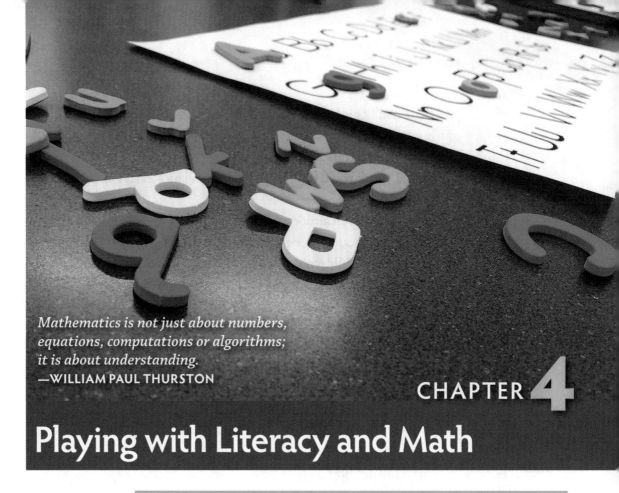

*Mathematics is not just about numbers,
equations, computations or algorithms;
it is about understanding.*
—WILLIAM PAUL THURSTON

CHAPTER 4

Playing with Literacy and Math

here is no way all those letters could hang on that tiny tree!"
I was reading the book *Chicka Chicka Boom Boom* (Martin and Archambault 1989) during circle time. This was a favorite for many, and the children always appreciated the comical story and catchy, rhyming verses. Toward the end of the story, most of the letters of the alphabet climb onto a tree before tumbling back to the ground. It was at this point in the story that Julia questioned the plausibility of the situation and shouted out her opinion.

"Yeah, no way! I mean, how can all those letters fit up there? How would they even climb? They have no legs!" Julia's classmates nodded their heads in agreement and voiced their opinions too.

"How big would that tree have to be? There are a lot of letters in the alphabet!"

"More if there are upper- *and* lowercase letters mixed together."

"That would be over a hundred letters on one tree!"

FIGURE 4.1
Children use an alphabet chart to help them calculate how many letters are included in a favorite children's book.

"No, I don't think there are that many letters in the alphabet. Not one hundred. That's too many."

"How many letters are there?"

"Well, I think you'd have to double them since each letter can be big and small."

"How big do you think each letter is?"

And in that moment a new math inquiry was sparked. I was interested in how the children's previous experiences with quantity and measurement were emerging in this conversation. Some children were interested in the idea of doubling to figure out how many upper- and lowercase letters there are. Others were considering the size the tree needed to be to hold that many letters and wondering about proportional reasoning as they compared the size of the letters to the tree. Before returning to reading, I asked the children to consider how big the tree would need to be to hold all the letters.

Building on Children's Ideas

CHILDREN ARRIVE at their first year of school with a myriad of experiences and ideas that shape the way they observe and interpret the world around them. And while school often encourages us to view each subject in its own isolated box, children do not naturally view their surroundings in this way. When children decide to make a treasure map, invent a game, or pretend to work in a grocery store, they draw upon their many understandings about how the world works. In school, we can build on these schemas, helping our students develop as they talk, read, write, and mathematize the world around them. We can meet students where they are in their understanding and use both planned and spontaneous moments to help them develop important literacy and math understandings through play.

FIGURE 4.2
A child draws shapes on a large chalkboard displayed in the schoolyard.

Clipboard Portfolios: Drawing, Writing, and Talking About Mathematics

Wow! You got another point!" Josh motions toward where a chip has landed in a bowl. He glances down at his paper. "That means that you have five!"

"Yep! I think I'm winning!" Mia uses tally marks to record her points. She looks at Josh's side of the T-chart and taps the tallies with her pencil. "One, two, three . . . You have three points. I have two more than you!"

Josh and Mia are playing a game on the carpet using small catapults made from wooden clothespins. Each foam chip they successfully launch from their clothespin catapult onto a target earns them a point. Next to the two children is a clipboard with paper where they record their score using tallies on a T-chart—a system of their own choosing. When their game is interrupted by a special event, Josh and Mia store the T-chart on Josh's clipboard to come back to later, when they can continue their game.

THE CLASS recently learned about T-charts during a whole-group activity. After demonstrating several examples of authentic ways T-charts are used, I invited students to try this way of organizing information. "You might try a T-chart like the ones we've looked at or you might think of a new way to use a T-chart. If you do try out a T-chart, make sure to let us know so you can share it and we can all learn from what you've done." With just this fairly brief introduction, many students eagerly took on the challenge, confidently incorporating T-charts into different aspects of their play.

The T-chart is just one of many graphic organizing tools that children can use to support their mathematical thinking. Writing and drawing are important parts of math, both for communicating our thinking to others and for processing our own ideas. In our writing center, each child has their own clipboard, stored for easy access on a freestanding wooden bookshelf (see Figure 4.3). Children can retrieve their clipboards at any time during the day and use them as needed to support an activity. In addition to blank paper, other paper choices are available in baskets in the writing center. Children may choose to use a T-chart to create a survey, use bullet points to make a list, use lined paper to write a letter, use a Venn diagram to compare two things, or use grid paper to make a map. After I introduce a graphic organizer during a short whole-group lesson, I add copies of it to the writing area and remind children that they are free to try it out. We start slowly in the beginning of the year with blank paper and build the collection of templates over time. Children

FIGURE 4.3
Each child in our class has a clipboard that is easily accessible on a wooden bookshelf.

FIGURE 4.4
"Do you like the way the gardenia smells?" A child creates a survey for his peers to respond to and places it near a vase of flowers.

become more creative and confident through repeated experiences. They also share their work with one another during our sharing circle at the end of choice time, which often inspires other children to attempt something similar the next day.

Our clipboards get a lot of use during choice time. Often children will incorporate math thinking into their writing as they use their clipboards to support their roles in play situations. For example, children playing in the house center might create a grocery list. They carefully copy fruit and vegetable vocabulary cards placed at the center and record how many of each they need to buy (e.g., 2 melons, 6 bananas). In order to highlight and extend this thinking, I sometimes play alongside the children, taking on the roles they assign me (e.g., a mom, the cashier at the store). I use this time to notice and wonder about their play, which often reflects their mathematical thinking: "Can you help me figure out how much money I need to get out of my wallet for these groceries?" "Hey, this line is only for people with ten items or less. Do you have more than that?" "You put one hundred apples on your grocery list! What will you do with all of those apples?"

Other times, children use the clipboards and a T-chart to survey their peers (see Figure 4.4). After crafting a question with two possible answers, they make their way through the classroom, asking peers to record their names on either side of the T-chart to indicate their response. Children then excitedly total each side to see which option is most popular. There is a great sense of ownership and power in creating and carrying out a survey. Children choose the questions that are most interesting to them: Do you want to come to my birthday party? Do you like dogs? Did you wear a hat to school? They are invested in the outcome of the surveys in ways that sometimes surprise adults. *You* may not have a strong urge to find out who in the class prefers slugs or snails—but a child might! Children are often eager to share the results of their surveys, and we make time in our sharing circle to do this frequently. Often, the work of one child inspires other children to create their own survey.

Another popular activity is creating detailed "treasure maps" at the writing center and then bringing the map outside during recess. Children follow the directions and then record additional information on their maps (e.g., landmarks in the yard, animals, directional arrows). These map-making and map-following experiences give children meaningful opportunities to use positional words (e.g., next to, above, below, inside, outside), read, write, problem solve, and revise their ideas.

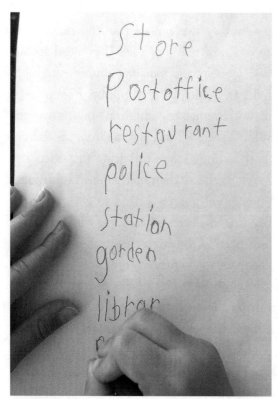

FIGURE 4.5
Before going on a neighborhood walk, a child creates a list of all the institutions in our local community that might use math.

Although children often use the clipboards independently to support math and literacy explorations in their play, we also use them in whole-group activities. For example, before venturing outside on one of our regular community walks, I often ask children to predict what they might observe (e.g., birds, signs, cars) and record these predictions on their clipboards. As we take our walk, children scout for the anticipated objects, making tally marks next to each item they see. At the end of the walk, children can total and compare their results.

Having a clipboard for each child also facilitates the public sharing of literacy and numeracy work. Each week I ask children to choose a piece of drawing or writing that they are proud of to display on the top of their clipboards for the week. As their work accumulates, it's interesting for children to flip through and see the progression of their ideas. Clipboards are stored face out on the shelf, so it's easy for children to browse one another's work. It's also a convenient way for me to quickly notice the work children have been engaged in with their clipboards and choose pieces to highlight with the whole class or small groups of children. For example, when two children wanted to create a survey with many answer choices rather than just two as they had previously done, we looked to other children's work for models of how they might organize that data.

Many times, children ask to share what's on their clipboard during our sharing circles. With experience, they become more confident in articulating the process behind their writing and drawing and in asking deeper questions of one another. Children often self-select what they would like to share, but I also ask children to bring specific work to our sharing circle. This allows me to highlight relevant math thinking and share it with the whole class. Selecting children's work to share also means that I can "slow down" our thinking, lingering on a particular idea. I can model open-ended questions and encourage children to delve more deeply into explaining their math thinking and engaging in the thinking of others. Let's drop in on one of these sharing-time conversations, in which the class is questioning Sawyer about a detailed map he has made of a Mario game.

Sawyer points to his picture as he explains the work on his clipboard during sharing circle (see Figure 4.6). "See—it's a game! You need to go through the secret passage and jump over the trap or you'll get caught!" The other children appear quite interested in Sawyer's drawing and raise their hands to ask questions. They are curious to know more about how his games works, and many make connections to experiences they have had playing games at home. He calls on them one at a time.

"What are the characters' names?"

"How do you earn points in your game?"

"This is like a game my brother plays. Can more than one person play?"

FIGURE 4.6
Sawyer's labeled map of a game includes traps and secret passages.

"What happens in the next level? Did you draw that picture yet?"

"Where do you record the points for each character?"

An excited chatter hums throughout the group. During the next choice time, I notice that many children are drawing their own unique games using their clipboards. As a way of extending their mapping and storytelling work, I invite those who have finished their drawings to recreate them three-dimensionally using blocks and other loose parts at the building center. Moving between two- and three-dimensional representations allows children to develop important visual-spatial reasoning as well as providing them with an opportunity to actually "play" their game as they maneuver mini-figures through mazes and calculate and compare points earned.

A CLIPBOARD seems like a simple tool. And yet, in our classroom clipboards allow children a space in which they can explore their own ideas and investigate their own questions. Children can save their work to refer to and share their work with their peers. Choice and ownership are critical to children's development as readers, writers, and mathematicians, and the clipboard, in all its simplicity, can help students foster these identities and build literacy and math understandings.

Literacy-Inspired STEAM Challenges

During choice time, a small group of children gathered around the water table. A few minutes later I noticed more children headed over to that area and heard the excited voices of those gathered there. I walked over to investigate.

Earlier in the day we had read *The Gingerbread Man*. The children were an enthusiastic audience for this well-loved book, laughing along with the Gingerbread Man's antics and chanting the familiar phrase: "Run, run as fast as you can. You can't catch me, I'm the Gingerbread Man!"

As I came closer to the water-table play, I noticed that the children had designed and built a boat using wooden craft sticks and were attempting to float a paper Gingerbread Man across the water. Curious about their ideas, I asked the students to explain what they were doing.

"We were worried about the Gingerbread Man! We don't want him to ask the fox for help crossing the water, because we all know how that ends! We're making him a boat so that he doesn't need the fox!" I watched as the children gently placed a paper Gingerbread Man that someone had drawn into the craft-stick boat and gently pushed it toward the middle of the water table. Water quickly seeped in through holes in the side of the boat, and in just a few moments the Gingerbread Man was soaked. The boat then slowly sank to the bottom of the water table.

"We need more tape! The sticks aren't close enough together!" Emme shared excitedly.

"No, I think that this boat isn't good because the sides aren't high enough. We need it to be bigger," Jazz argued.

"If it's bigger it will sink because it will be heavy. It needs to be smaller!" pointed out Niko.

The children continued offering suggestions for what went wrong with their plan and what the next step might be for building a better boat. For the next few days, groups of children spent their choice time planning and building a variety of boats, using materials from around the classroom. As they worked, the children tested and evaluated boat designs, paying careful attention to the size and shape of the boats. They used their observations to help revise their plans, reflecting upon what had worked in their previous trials and how to proceed going forward in order to create the perfect boat for the Gingerbread Man. When the children tired of this activity during indoor play, I sparked interest in it again by bringing boat-making materials outside on a rainy afternoon. Children used their boat-making schema to create "puddle boats" that could float and carry pebbles down the walkway.

FIGURE 4.7
A question is displayed next to blocks, inviting the children to explore growing patterns.

STEAM IS an acronym that stands for science, technology, engineering, art, and math. STEAM-inspired experiences promote critical thinking and the integration of twenty-first-century competencies through hands-on explorations (see Figure 4.7). During these STEAM inquiries, children are invited to solve an open-ended problem. They identify questions or problems and then research and investigate possible solutions. Revision plays a key role in most STEAM-inspired experiences, as children make changes to their initial ideas based on previous attempts to solve the problem.

In our classroom, we often use favorite picture books and fairy tales as STEAM sparks. Here are some questions I might ask the students:

- ◆ How can you help the three Billy Goats Gruff build a troll-proof bridge?

- ◆ How can you create a soft landing for Humpty Dumpty to fall on so that he won't break?

- ◆ How can you design a system for retrieving water for Jack and Jill so they don't have to keep walking up the hill?

- ◆ How can you keep Peter's snowball (from Ezra Jack Keats' *The Snowy Day* [1976]) from melting in his pocket when he comes inside?

- ◆ How can you design a dragon-proof outfit for Elizabeth in *The Paper Bag Princess* (Munsch 2009)?

Sometimes these are questions that have emerged in our conversations during circle time, and other times I invite children to explore problems and materials that I have organized.

STEAM challenges often emerge spontaneously during play when children encounter unexpected problems. Such an experience occurred when our class was playing outside and noticed a duck's nest. Children worked together to create a protective barrier to keep the duck nest safe from people who might accidentally harm it. As they worked, the children discussed which materials (all found outside) they would use and how they might stack these materials to create a strong barrier.

In our classroom, STEAM challenges often emerge as a result of questions or concerns that children experience—either through real-life situations or through empathetic connections with characters in a story. Children become emotionally invested in unresolved issues and are inspired to help in some way. Here are the inspirations for some of our favorite STEAM experiences:

- ◆ Worried that Hansel and Gretel would be eaten by the witch, children created a pulley system to help them move undetected across the forest.

- Scared that the princess would be locked forever in a tall tower, children designed and created a tool to help her open the door when she didn't have a key.

- Wishing for a pot of gold, children designed and created leprechaun traps to leave in the classroom overnight.

- Hoping to help the Three Little Pigs, the children designed a wolf-proof house.

- Upset over a fruit fly infestation in the room upon returning from spring break, the children researched, designed, and tested traps to catch the flies.

- Worried that the new spring bulbs emerging in front of the school would be stepped on, the children designed and built a protective barrier.

- Eager to deliver letters to one another at the writing center, the children built a mailbox system with enough slots for everyone in the class.

- Concerned about mud being tracked into the cubby room during spring weather, the children brainstormed and built devices to clean the mud off their boots without dirtying their hands.

- Disappointed that a favorite toy truck had lost a wheel, the children problem solved how to fix it using loose parts from the art area.

- Eager to collect as much candy as possible while trick-or-treating, the children designed a large bag for Halloween night.

- Curious about how Santa's reindeer pulled such a heavy sleigh, the children brainstormed how to create harnesses that would help lighten their load.

STEAM activities can encourage complex problem solving and perseverance that transfer across children's interests and across subject areas. STEAM activities that are inspired by literacy experiences reinforce students' storytelling and comprehension skills as they retell the story, consider characters' feelings and motivations, or imagine alternative endings to favorite stories.

When children encounter questions or problems in their play that require action, we, as teachers, should try to resist the urge to provide immediate answers. Instead, we can encourage students to collaborate to solve a problem. We can help students learn to listen to and encourage one another through shared curiosity and inquiry. Teachers can support students in these inquiries by listening to children's wonderings and taking them seriously. We can question students and direct them to materials and resources that assist them in problem solving. And, of course, we can celebrate their discoveries and provide a forum for them to share their findings and new questions.

Using Picture Books and Illustrations to Inspire Math Exploration

One year, the children in our classroom became fascinated by the spiders they found living in our schoolyard. Hoping to spark more thinking on this topic, I placed a collection of fiction and nonfiction books about spiders in the reading area. One book, *I Love Spiders*, by John Parker (1988), particularly captured the children's interest. As they read the text, they named and described the spiders they saw in the illustrations.

"Look! Those are all small spiders. Those are like the ones I saw on the logs outside."

"These ones are different colors—red and blue. I've never seen a red or blue spider before!"

"Ew! These ones have really long legs like the daddy longlegs my brother found in his room!"

"These ones all have little eyes. How many eyes do spiders have in real life?"

"This giant spider is like one hundred of those tiny ones."

Hoping to build on the students' interest in spiders and the mathematical language with which they had described them, I displayed the book to the class during our next morning meeting and asked the

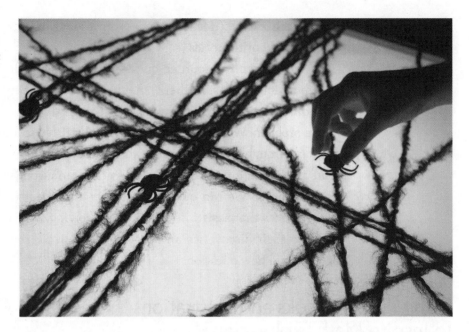

students to share math questions they might have about the illustrations: "How many legs are there altogether for all spiders on this page?" "How long would a length of silk need to be for a spider's entire web?" "How high do you think those spiders can jump?" Children also began to construct their own webs outside using yarn affixed to tree stumps, creating mini-playscapes for imaginative play.

Picture books like *I Love Spiders* have the potential to connect readers to real and imagined characters and settings while offering rich contexts to explore mathematical ideas. There are multiple benefits to using illustrations to inspire mathematical thinking, including providing a relevant and meaningful problem to explore, increasing children's motivation and participation in the activities, promoting critical thinking, and increasing problem solving through relatable and emotionally connected situations (Burns 2005; Haury 2001). Illustrations and photographs are accessible and provide an opportunity for all students to notice, name, and wonder mathematically.

There are times in our classroom when we go many days without a rich inquiry to explore; the children's attention and interest won't settle for more than a day or two on any topic, and I need something to inspire them. In these situations, I often invite students to engage with questions inspired by a book, a photo, or an illustration. Providing tools and materials to investigate these questions often leads children to extend the provocation, asking and investigating their own questions as well.

Think back to the vignette that opened this chapter. After reading the book *Chicka Chicka Boom Boom*, the children in our class were still curious about the fictional math situation. They continued to wonder about how big a tree would have to be to hold fifty-two letters, and how the letters would hang from the tree. I resisted the urge to jump in with my own ideas of how to explore this scenario mathematically and instead asked the children to reflect upon how they might like to solve the problem. At the conclusion of our whole-group discussion, the children appeared stuck. They restated their questions, retelling the story, but did not have a clear direction for how they might proceed. I reminded them to keep their wonderings fresh in their minds as they moved into choice time, and to be on the lookout for materials in our classroom that might help in our work regarding the letters and the tree.

A short time later I was approached by two children, Holden and Zaid, with a plastic tree. Materials like trees, grass, animals, and vehicles are included in the construction center to invite dramatic storytelling while building, and the children had discovered the tree while playing there.

Holden handed me the tree. "This tree reminds me of the one from the book. It's even the same type."

"And look! Here are some letters!" Zaid held a basket of tiny magnetic letters from the writing center. "They might fit on the tree!"

I invited the two boys to retrieve *Chicka Chicka Boom Boom* so they could revisit the story and examine the illustrations more carefully. The boys turned to one of the final pages in the book. The illustration depicts the tree bending over from the weight of so many letters.

"I think we could try to hang some of these letters on our tree and see if they fit! Maybe we can figure out if all the letters can hang on the tree at once!" said Holden. The boys set to work on the carpet, looking through the bin to find matching sets of upper- and lowercase letters.

Eager to see if I could extend the children's curiosity about the story further, I created a math invitation to place on a table for the next day. I found a slightly larger tree from the toy bin and displayed the book next to the tree, clipping it open to the page showing the tree bending from the weight of all the letters. I included a basket with alphabet beads, pipe cleaners, and scissors. I was curious to see if the children would find ways of affixing the letters to the tree. I included drawing materials, hoping that the children might record their observations. Later that day, during choice time, I observed the children exploring the center. Their continued interest in the book facilitated many learning opportunities: counting out sets of matching letters, cutting the pipe cleaners into different sizes, using the materials to hang the beads in the tree, and engaging in math conversations as they connected their work to the book:

"I found more letters than you did! My pile is bigger!"

"I am spelling my name with the letters. I have six."

"I needed three long pieces and two short pieces of pipe cleaners to attach my letters to the tree."

"I wish we had another two trees. That's how many we'd need to hold all of the letters in the bowl."

I was thrilled to see so much learning emerge from the spontaneous book discussion.

Photographs as Math Provocations

In preparing for choice time one day, I place a number of large, colorful photos of objects from around our classroom (see Figure 4.9). I include photos that feature objects I know the children will find irresistible—animals, vehicles, toys—in order to draw their attention to the activity. I also include interesting photos from books we have read. Pages are covered with plastic protectors so that children can write directly on them with dry erase markers without damaging the book. As the children explore and talk with one another about the photos, I sit down at the table next to them. Listening to their noticings and wonderings, I highlight mathematical connections and add some of my own questions.

FIGURE 4.9
A child writes an equation to describe how he calculated the number of Legos in this picture.

Isla notices a picture of colorful koi fish in a pond. She immediately begins counting them but keeps losing her place. She is not sure if she is counting the same fish twice. Noticing her frustration, I invite her to write on the photo as a strategy for organizing her count. As she counts, she writes each number she says directly on the fish.

"There!" she says as she finishes. "Now I can see there are seven fish."

"Look, you can circle them too!" Evie is sitting next to Isla, watching her work. "You can put them into groups—two, two, two and one. Two plus two plus two plus one equals seven."

LIKE BOOK ILLUSTRATIONS, photos are often hooks for children's interests. Families can be asked to send in photos of interesting objects or scenarios, inviting their participation in this experience. Photos can also be taken from around the classroom, the neighborhood, or students' homes. With practice, children can take their own photos to be printed out and shared at the writing center for other children to explore.

Consider offering some photographs that hint at a story to be told. Children can use these photos to tell their own stories about what *might* be happening in the photo. For example, a photo of dogs might inspire a story like this: "Two dogs were lost, and then they found another group of eight dogs, and they all became friends. Now there are ten dogs in the group!" Telling their own stories related to the photos helps students develop the kind of math language they may encounter in story problems during math class; but perhaps more importantly, it helps them craft their own ideas and questions.

In addition to telling number stories verbally, some students may show interest in representing their stories with equations. Picture books and photos provide a meaningful context for them to explore the different ways a story problem can be represented. For example, after examining a photo of nine cats, Carm wondered how she and her three friends might share the cats if they were real. Her math question became "How can four friends share these cats?" She decided to draw directly on the photo to help her solve the problem. She circled four unequal groups of cats (1, 2, 3, 3) and then wrote an addition sentence to describe her thinking ("1 + 2 + 3 + 3"). During sharing circle Carm showed her peers the picture, explaining her math question and how she decided to solve the problem. Some of the other children noted that it wouldn't be fair because the children in Carm's story did not each receive an equal number of cats. They wondered how nine cats could be shared equally among the four friends, leading to an interesting discussion about whether this was mathematically possible. The more practice children have generating their own contextualized problems, the more flexible they become when working with numbers and number relationships. Encourage students to work together and talk about their problems, and celebrate the unique stories and solutions that students come up with.

Serving Up Math with Modeling Dough

During choice time, I heard a commotion and looked over to a nearby table. There were several children grabbing for the large ball of freshly made modeling dough in Emeline's hands. Before intervening, I watched to see why the children were upset. "I need some too!" Lily shouted at Emeline. "You've got too much!"

"Yeah, please share!" Tyler said as he tried to pull some of the dough from Emeline's hands.

"Hey! Stop it! I helped make it so I should get the most!" Emeline asserted as she backed away from the table, cradling the ball against her body.

"You're getting it all over your shirt," Jay responded. "Plus, that's not fair. Why do you get all the dough? We should all get some."

FIGURE 4.10
A child divides modeling dough into eight slices of "pizza" to share with her friends.

Curious about Jay's suggestion and eager to refocus this disagreement on productive problem solving, I approached the table. "It seems like a lot of people would like to sculpt today," I observed. "I like Jay's suggestion. I wonder how you can make sure everyone gets a fair, or equal, amount of dough." The children looked at one another.

"Oh, I know!" Emeline chirped as she placed the ball of dough on the table and began flattening it out into a circular shape. "We fight over pizza all the time at my house. My brothers eat way too much. My mom makes us count the number of slices and then divide them evenly so we all get the same number. Let's turn this dough into pizza!"

"But I'm not hungry and I don't want to make pizza," Lily pouted. "I just want to play with dough."

"You don't have to pretend it's pizza," Emeline replied. "We're just doing that to figure out how much to give everyone."

"Oh, okay," Lily answered as she watched Emeline use a cutter to divide the pizza into eight pieces.

IN OUR CLASSROOM, modeling dough is a staple material that the children are free to sculpt and manipulate. A table is set aside during choice time for modeling dough exploration. Sometimes we make the dough together in our school kitchen, and other times we ask for family volunteers to create the dough at home and send it to school. (Each year in September we poll families to see who might be interested in helping out.) The dough, along with many interesting tools (e.g., cutters, mashers, pans, child-friendly knives, rolling pins, trays) and materials (e.g., feathers, pebbles, gems, googly eyes, craft sticks), is housed on a shelf for easy retrieval. In our classroom, we often associate modeling dough with literacy and art for many reasons:

◆ Modeling dough is a cost-effective and open-ended art material that can be made together with the children and used in many different projects both indoors and out.

◆ Modeling dough helps children develop fine-motor muscles in their hands, preparing them for detailed writing and drawing experiences.

◆ Working with modeling dough side by side with peers leads to productive oral language experiences. Children may explain how they are manipulating the dough (e.g., pounding, smashing, rolling, pinching) or give directions to one another for making something: "First you need to roll the ball flat. Then you pick a cutter. Next you press it into the dough to make a cookie. Then you put it on the tray."

◆ Children learn that the process of sculpting with the dough is just as important as the finished product, if not more so, and that their creations can be continually revised.

◆ Working with modeling dough can be a calming sensory experience for many, especially if texture and scent are added (e.g., loose parts, dried flowers, spices, cocoa, coffee grinds, sparkles, food coloring, essential oils).

Over the years, I have learned that working with modeling dough can also spark many rich math experiences. Sometimes I design learning experiences around specific curricular goals. For example, when problem solving with fractions, we might pretend that we need to share six cookies equally among four friends. Other times the math naturally emerges from the children's interactions, as when Emeline divided the dough into equal-sized pieces after making a connection to sharing pizza at home with her family. Rolling up your sleeves and playing alongside children in the modeling dough center is the best way to highlight the math thinking children are already engaged in and nudge them to investigate new questions.

Make Play dough
Scented?

These are some of the invitations to work with modeling dough we've offered in our classroom:

◆ When we made modeling dough for the first time in our classroom, I posted the recipe on a large piece of chart paper so that we could refer to it as we added and mixed ingredients. We discussed measurement tools, compared the different amounts of ingredients, and discussed the order of actions taken in the recipe. Later, children also used the chart-paper recipe when pretending in the dramatic arts "house center." A copy of the recipe was included in our September newsletter so families could make and enjoy modeling dough together at home.

◆ When I included clean rubber number stampers (traditionally used with ink) in the modeling dough center, children pressed the numbers into the dough in different sequences (e.g., by ones, twos, fives) (see Figures 4.11 and 4.12). Adding Legos to the center promoted counting skills such as one-to-one correspondence and matching quantities with numerals—for example, a Lego with six pegs corresponded with the numeral 6.

◆ Adding different sizes of trays, tins, plates, and bowls inspired children to pretend they were cooks preparing for a big feast. Children considered measurement ideas as they lined and filled the containers with the "food" they had created.

◆ Adding various sizes and shapes of seasonal cutters helped children classify, sort, and order the "cookies" they pressed from the dough.

◆ Including recipe books, writing pads, and play money inspired children to transform the center into a bakery, where they used math in a meaningful context (e.g., recording numbers of objects, paying for items and making change, and making up their own recipes).

◆ Repurposing kitchen utensils as sculpting tools (e.g., potato masher, spatula, flipper, garlic press) prompted the children to create interesting prints and patterns in the dough.

FIGURE 4.11
Rubber stampers can be used to press numbers into modeling dough.

FIGURE 4.12
Children explore stamping Legos in modeling dough and matching the number of pegs to the numerals on the stamps.

FIGURE 4.13
A plastic toddler toy leaves an interesting design when rolled in the modeling dough.

◆ Using dramatic props such as birthday candles helped children represent quantity when pretending the dough was a cake and role-playing a birthday party.

◆ Repurposing interesting toddler toys (e.g., sensory balls) as tools that can be rolled in the dough encouraged children to create and name interesting shapes and patterned lines (see Figure 4.13).

◆ Adding natural objects (e.g., leaves, pine cones, acorn caps) that can be pressed in the dough helped children mathematize what they saw (e.g., patterns in the veins of a leaf and the circular nature of acorn caps).

◆ Modeling language in context helped children discover, compare, and contrast their individual creations. For example, I might say, "The modeling dough worm you are rolling is much longer than mine." Or I might observe, "Lindsey's ladybug has six spots on it, but yours has only four."

BASIC MODELING DOUGH RECIPE

Ingredients:

2 cups flour

2 tablespoons oil

½ cup salt

2 tablespoons cream of tartar

1½ cups boiling water

Food coloring (optional)

Directions:

1. In a large bowl, combine flour, salt, and cream of tartar. Whisk together until mixed well.
2. Gently stir in the oil.
3. In a large measuring cup, add food coloring to the hot water if you are coloring the dough. Take care when handling hot water, especially if children are helping to make the dough.
4. Carefully and slowly pour the hot water into the bowl with the flour mixture. Use a sturdy wooden spoon to begin mixing the dough.
5. When the dough has cooled enough to be touched, knead the dough (in the bowl or on a clean counter) with your hands until well blended.
6. Enhance the dough with other interesting ingredients that might add texture, scent, and color (e.g., coffee grinds, spices, sand, fresh chopped herbs).
7. Enjoy!

Modeling dough is one tool we can use to encourage students to process and express thinking that reinforces and extends both literacy and math ideas. As children work in the modeling dough center, they build on the learning that is happening throughout the school day, intermingling storytelling with mathematical problem solving.

Using Building Experiences to Uncover Math and Literacy

One afternoon during choice time Preston was building with small wooden blocks on the carpet. After adding a few blocks to his structure, he stood up and took a few steps back so he could take a good look at his creation. "No, that's not right. That's not it.

FIGURE 4.14
Preston references a photo to help him recreate the Ambassador Bridge with blocks.

It's missing something." Overhearing his words, I approached the carpet to learn more.

"What are you building today?" I asked.

"It's supposed to be the Ambassador Bridge, but it doesn't look right. We drove over it last weekend when we went to the Detroit Zoo. It's got big posts in the middle with long cables, but I don't remember exactly what it looks like."

I smiled. The children had been interested in exploring bridges lately, and I was excited to see Preston focusing on a local landmark. The Ambassador Bridge is a busy border crossing, and many of the children had traveled across it when visiting the United States.

"Why don't we do a bit of research?" I prompted. "We could look up photos online to help with your design, and we could see if there are books about suspension bridges in the library so you can understand how the cables work."

"A suspension bridge?" Preston asked.

"Yes, the Ambassador Bridge is a suspension bridge, which means that the deck where you drive is supported by cables."

"Wow!" Preston's eyes opened wide. "But there were so many trucks when we drove on it. How can cables be strong enough to hold all those cars and trucks? How long are the cables? The bridge is so high up. How did they even build that bridge over the river?" Questions bubbled up as Preston wondered aloud.

"Let's start writing down your questions," I suggested. "Then after you build, we can investigate and learn more about how the bridge was built and how it works."

"Yeah!" nodded Preston. "And then after that I want to know all about the Detroit Tunnel. We're taking that to the Tigers game next week."

THE CONSTRUCTION CENTER is one of the busiest and most popular areas of our classroom. Children have access to many commercial building toys (e.g., wooden blocks, Legos, marble runs), repurposed items (e.g., paper tubes, carpet squares, tree cookies, frame corners), and loose parts (e.g., river rocks, shells, metal rings) for imaginative play. They are encouraged to collaborate on building large structures of their own design. Regular building opportunities support many areas of math. Here are some examples:

◆ spatial logic and reasoning

◆ sorting and classification

◆ shape and pattern understanding

◆ exploration of symmetry and balance

◆ problem solving

◆ measurement

Sometimes these math invitations are planned ahead of time, and teacher-provided materials and challenges are offered to students (e.g., Can you design a fence to keep rabbits out of the garden?). Other times the math occurs naturally in the context of free play (e.g., Why does our tower keep falling over?). Active participation in the center alongside the

FIGURE 4.15
*Sheer fabric hangs from the tree branches
for children to incorporate into their outdoor
building experiences.*

FIGURE 4.16
*Large, repurposed boxes are a great building
material to use outside.*

children can help educators recognize these opportunities, support children's problem-solving strategies, and observe and document meaningful learning for assessment purposes. Some of the most mathematically meaningful experiences we have had in the construction center can be easily introduced in any classroom with a few simple materials.

Building Shelters

The children love to build shelters using different materials. Large wooden blocks are versatile and wonderful for encouraging collaboration and big body movements but can be hard to find and costly to purchase. A few cost-effective and easy-to-gather building materials that I have observed children use over and over are extra hardwood flooring; large, empty cardboard boxes; and sheer curtains (see Figures 4.15 and 4.16). These materials can be gathered from stores, donated by families, and found in thrift shops. They can be used individually or combined with other building materials, and they are fun to use inside and out. After children design a structure on paper, they can build it, problem solving any challenges that arise along the way.

Sequencing Stories

In addition to providing opportunities for mathematical thinking, block creations inspire children to construct stories together, too. Once children have created something from blocks, they often use the structure to role-play a story. They may retell familiar stories from picture books we have read as a class, reenact personal lived experiences, or improvise scenarios they have invented. Children can become the characters themselves, playing inside large structures they have created, or they can create characters using small toys and items from around the room for smaller-scale play. Through play in the construction center, children engage in storytelling together, develop complex character relationships and plots, and consider cause and effect within the context of their story.

Creating Ramps and Pathways

Another favorite activity for children is creating ramps and pathways to transport toys and materials, including marbles, balls, and toy cars. Any kind of sturdy material can be used to make these ramps and pathways, and children are inventive in how they combine and attach various resources together. Constructing these runs is typically a collaborative experience in which children are motivated to overcome unanticipated obstacles. They demonstrate great perseverance and creativity in designing, creating, testing, and revising their plans. Working together often makes the activity more enjoyable and builds children's collective schemas as they draw upon one another's ideas in order to achieve the best-working design possible.

Literacy can be fostered both inside and outside of the classroom. Learning to effectively speak, read, and write is a thrilling developmental milestone for children! As educators, we can cultivate a safe and supportive space in which multiple literacies are embedded and the mathematical relevance and application of text is intentionally explored. By creating these spaces, we empower children as readers, writers, and mathematicians in order to bring their ideas to life in new and innovative ways!

Every child is born a naturalist. His eyes are, by nature, open to the glories of the stars, the beauty of the flowers, and the mystery of life.

—RITU GHATOUREY

CHAPTER 5

Bringing Math Learning Outdoors

One day rain formed a giant puddle on the playground. The children were curious about how to cross over. It was too big and deep to skip or jump over, but they were determined to reach the other side.

Mason decided to try using some of our loose building parts. He gathered pieces of wood and began laying them down, starting from one edge of the puddle. As he placed two pieces of wood side by side, he checked the edges of the wood to see whether it was tall enough to serve as a bridge.

"I don't know if the wood is high enough. If the puddle is deeper than the wood, then this won't work."

I observed Mason as he carefully placed the wood down and then stepped on each piece, watching to see if the water rose higher than the wood. I noted the math and problem solving that emerged in his thinking—he was mentally measuring as he considered the depth of

FIGURE 5.1
A child walks on a trail through the woods near her school, looking for different lengths of sticks along the path.

the water and whether it was deeper than the wood was tall. After a few minutes, some friends joined him. As each piece of wood was added, the children continued to test their design to see whether their feet stayed dry.

"We're making a bridge so we can cross!"

"I think we need at least ten more pieces to finish it."

"I don't know if it's going to be wide enough to step on with both feet."

The children continued to lay the wood pieces side by side and end to end. When they ran out of pieces, they were perplexed.

"We don't have enough to finish our bridge!"

They stood around chatting for many minutes, stepping on their bridge, counting the pieces they had arranged and then looking around the yard for any loose pieces of wood they might have missed.

"I know! Let's take half of the pieces and move them so that we can make the bridge longer! We'll just have to walk on it one kid at a time instead!"

The children realized that if they narrowed their bridge, they could double its length. The amount of wood they used hadn't changed but their thinking had, and they were able to complete a workable way of crossing the water. Success! The children spent the rest of their outdoor time racing one by one across the big puddle. They even tried driving the tricycles across it—a process that led to some new questions to investigate: How much does this bike weigh and how much weight can this wood hold? What do we do about the wood moving around when we drive the tricycles over it? How fast can we drive without causing the wood to shift and the tricycle to fly into the mud?

Children's outdoor play is full of mathematical possibility. This puddle-crossing experience motivated children to engage in spontaneous and robust math that incorporated measurement and problem solving.

THINK BACK to your own childhood experiences playing outside. Perhaps you recall the joyful feeling of squishing your toes in mud or walking barefoot on wet grass. How about the tantalizing smell of flowers in the garden as you picked them to make potions? Or perhaps instead you remember the patterned hum of busy traffic passing by on city streets. Did you notice the sounds of bird songs outside your window or take note of ants in sidewalk cracks as you walked to a neighborhood park? Or maybe instead you have memories of watching cornstalks growing in a field, feeling excited for the day when they would be taller than you and you could finally run and hide from your siblings, playing spooky games in the dusk on warm autumn nights. Regardless of whether you live in an urban or rural area, there is something magical about being outside, noticing and wondering about the world around you.

Just as our own childhood experiences might be very different from one another's, our schools' outdoor spaces are likely to be diverse as well. I hope that this chapter inspires you to consider the potential for outdoor math regardless of what your school's outdoor space looks like or how much outdoor time you have in your schedule. As educators, one of the most powerful actions we can take is to listen deeply to the observations and wonderings of children. This is as true of our work outside the classroom walls as it is of our work inside. When we provide space for students to notice, wonder, and explore outdoor spaces through a mathematical lens, we offer them an expanded notion of what math is and what it means to be a mathematician.

FIGURE 5.2
A girl rescues worms from a giant puddle. She notes the differences in their length as she picks each one up.

In this chapter, we will consider three categories of outdoor mathematical experiences: (1) open-ended invitations, (2) teacher-initiated explorations, and (3) inquiries over time. We will also consider common challenges to working outdoors with children—from finding space to time constraints to making sure we address grade-level standards. My hope is that you will both recognize the possibilities already available in your current space and schedule and begin to imagine new ideas you would like to explore going forward. You will also notice throughout this chapter that many of the scenarios and activities presented strongly incorporate aspects of science. Integrating math and science is an effective way for educators to bring their classroom learning outdoors, helping to fulfill additional programming expectations in an already busy school day.

Open-Ended Mathematical Invitations

One fall, after beginning our unit on measurement, I placed a mechanical scale in the schoolyard for children to explore. I purposely placed it near a large collection of seasonal pumpkins and gourds, hoping that the children would become intrigued and incorporate it into their play. We had been exploring different ways of measuring during our math lessons, and I was wondering whether the children might be curious about the purpose of the scale or apply some of what they had recently learned to their outdoor play. The children were immediately drawn to the scale. It was clear they had limited experience with this particular type of scale because they were unsure of what to do with it at first. Curious to see how they would problem solve, I stood close enough that I could hear their conversations but far enough away as not to be an immediate source of help for them. They investigated the scale by physically manipulating it in different ways—spinning it around, turning it over, and pushing down on it.

"I don't know what this thing is!" Maeve exclaimed to her peers as she pushed downward on the platform.

"Look! It's like a clock. It has a little arm that moves when I push on it," Annelise shared as she made a connection to the unfamiliar

FIGURE 5.3
A child measures the circumference of a gourd using connecting links.

object. "I think my grandma has something like that in her bathroom."

"Yes, mine does too! I like to jump on it when I visit. But it's not a clock. Clocks have two little arms. Let's put something on it." Luke quickly gathered a few small gourds from nearby and began piling them on the scale. "One, two, three, four," he counted as he filled the platform. "Let's pretend we are shopping! I'm going to buy lots of little pumpkins for Halloween! These are so heavy! Look at how that little line-thing moves when I put more on it! I need a big bag to put them in when I'm done."

THE CHILDREN spent the duration of their outdoor time placing various objects on the scale and seeing how far they could make the needle move. Together they made the connection that the heavier the object, the farther the needle would move. I documented their math observations, taking photos of their work and transcribing bits of their conversations on my notepad. As I watched them play, I reflected on the experience and mentally planned for how to incorporate more measurement opportunities into future explorations. I thought about my curriculum document and mentally noted the expectations that connected to this experience. I considered the children's questions and what additional measuring tools could be introduced in a similar fashion. I wondered about my own role in the children's play. Maybe I could role-play a grocery store customer and invite children to pretend they were workers who needed to fill a specific order by using the scale to measure out acorns and twigs. Perhaps next time we went on walk we could bring a kitchen food scale with us to weigh the various objects we found along the way. I wondered what the children would suggest if I asked them

FIGURE 5.4
The children turn a large piece of pegboard into a giant geoboard by using fixed screws and bolts as anchors for rubber bands. They use the outdoor geoboard to explore shapes and lines. Educators who are worried about a sharp edge can turn the screws inward. Golf tees also work well in place of the screws.

during our next whole-group circle time what else they thought we could do with the scale. Perhaps they would be interested in the overall size of each gourd and look for ways to measure the height and circumference of each. I jotted these reflections down alongside my notes on the children's work. I wanted to remember them later on when planning for the rest of the measurement unit.

Open-ended invitations, like the scale and the gourds, consist of teacher- or child-provided materials that encourage children to develop and investigate their own questions through mathematical play. These materials can be set out as a center in a central outdoor location for children to use in innovative ways. Providing interesting measuring tools such as different kinds of scales or rulers, a variety of building materials including sticks and blocks, math tools such as dice and dominoes, or a pegboard with screws and bolts (see Figure 5.4) entices children to be creative in the ways in which they interact with the materials. There is still intentionality behind the teacher's choices (if scales or rulers are provided, an educator might be hoping children use them to measure in some way); however, the ways in which the children play with the tools will shape the direction of the experience.

McDonald (2018) recommends that educators play numerous roles when first observing and then joining children in an open-ended play experience. At first educators are *observers*, noticing what is happening in an open-ended situation and documenting what they see by taking photos of children and recording anecdotal observations. They then transform into *instructional leaders*, who ask questions to nudge children's mathematical thinking. As the activity unfolds, educators can then become *participants* in the activity or game alongside the children, sharing their own thinking at times, but also focusing on listening deeply and responding to the children's ideas.

Listening to Children and Following Their Questions

FIGURE 5.5

After a very rainy day during which one child's boots got stuck in the mud, students were inspired to ask the question, "How can we measure how deep the mud puddles are?"

*I*t had rained all day. In the afternoon, the rain finally stopped, and we were able to head outdoors. A giant puddle had formed in the center of the asphalt. Fortunately, in our classroom, we have a collection of gently used rain boots, and a pair was provided for each child to wear in order to explore the puddles. Thrilled by the giant puddle, the children stomped and splashed off to play in the water. Many enjoyed the experience of just running and jumping, seeing how big of a splash they could make. Others were happy using cups and bowls to scoop and pour the muddy water as they prepared pretend hot chocolate for everyone to enjoy on the soggy day. As I often do, I took a moment to stand back and observe the children. I was curious to see what questions and ideas would develop through their play. And as I listened to the children's conversations, I recognized many math questions in their explorations. "How much water had actually fallen from the sky?" they wondered. "Was there even a way to measure all the water?" "How much water could they scoop during the time they were outside?" "How deep was the puddle?" "How long would it take to skip across the entire puddle?" "How many boots fit into the puddle?" "Who could make the biggest splash?" I recorded their questions in my anecdotal notes journal and took some photos of their play. Not wanting to interrupt them, I planned to bring their questions and the photos to our next whole-group discussion on the carpet. I wondered how they might suggest investigating some of these questions and hoped to revisit these ideas during our next outdoor play, since the water would not be drying up anytime soon. I considered what aspect of our math curriculum might be fulfilled through further exploration of the puddles and how I could extend these ideas during indoor math activities. Perhaps children would be interested in exploring measuring at the water table if I helped them see the connection between the water in our schoolyard and the sensory materials available indoors.

While splashing through puddles with rain boots is an exciting invitation to mathematize, this experience may not be practical for all school settings. I tell this story to point out that young children are often thrilled by outdoor experiences that may seem ordinary to adults. When given the opportunity, they ask mathematical questions about the world around them that we, as adults, might not think of. "How many new mushrooms will we see after a rainy day?" "How far can I jump from this step?" "What kinds of collections of outdoor treasures can I find today?" "Why does that snail move so slow?" "How many ants live in that anthill?" "How many branches are on that big tree?" When we learn to listen to children and follow up on mathematical lines of inquiry, we acknowledge and affirm their natural inclination to connect nature and math and to be curious about their world.

FIGURE 5.6
Finding treasures in the yard leads to math thinking as children classify, sort, count, and make patterns with the objects.

FIGURE 5.7
Noticing natural events such as worms washing up on the pavement after a hard rain can inspire math thinking as children wonder about the number of worms they collect, how long they are, and how fast they can move.

FIGURE 5.8
Nature offers beautiful ways to explore math as children wonder about the colors and patterns they observe on creatures like birds and butterflies.

Creating a "Wonder Wagon":
An Open-Ended Invitation to Mathematize

OPEN-ENDED invitations empower children to choose the direction of their play and can spark deeper inquiries along the way. And while few commercial materials are needed for successful outside play, it does help to be prepared with some tools that can inspire children's imagination. Each year I create a Wonder Wagon full of math goodies that can be easily wheeled to any spot in the schoolyard or pulled along by the children for community walks and visits to local parks, farmer's markets, and nature sanctuaries. Over the years I've included various materials in our Wonder Wagon. Here are some examples:

FIGURE 5.9

Writing materials, such as chart paper and a bucket of crayons, can be hung on wire fencing using metal hooks, creating an invitation for children to record their observations and ideas in the natural world.

- Clipboards
- Thermometers
- Sketch pads
- Paper (chart paper, loose-leaf paper)
- Metal hooks (for hanging writing materials on the fence)
- Buckets
- Writing utensils (pencils, markers, crayons)
- Measuring tools (rulers, yardsticks, measuring tapes)
- Connecting cubes or links
- A large plastic or fabric number line
- Sorting trays (easily made from repurposed wooden boxes or clear plastic fruit trays)
- Sorting hoops
- Various shades of paint chips or a color wheel

FIGURE 5.10
A group of children match wildflower petals they find on a walk to paint chips.

◆ Magnifying glasses

◆ Tweezers

◆ Scissors

◆ Repurposed frames or trays

◆ Math tools such as laminated five frames, ten frames, Venn diagrams

◆ A large blanket

◆ Scales (digital and balance)

◆ Timers (digital and sand)

Of course, you don't have to have all these materials to get started. Choose a few tools your students might like to start with and continue adding to your Wonder Wagon throughout the year. If you don't have access to a wagon, use a large basket or box instead. Additional baskets of teacher-initiated games and supplemental activities can be placed in the wagon or scattered around the outdoor space as needed. Often my class brings activities we have been exploring during indoor choice time outdoors—the change in scenery and freedom that fresh air and large spaces provide encourage children to explore the materials in new ways.

The following are open-ended invitations I have found particularly productive for mathematical conversations. You might use these exactly as they are, revise them to bring out an important mathematical idea in your standards, or design new open-ended mathematical invitations based on your students' interests and standards.

REPURPOSED RUNS

Suggested Materials: Repurposed floorboards, tubes, cardboard tubes, gutter pieces, metal hooks, rolling toys (e.g., marbles, cars, balls), writing materials including paper and crayons.

What's the Math? Describe and compare measurable attributes; develop a plan for problem solving and revise ideas based on previous experiences and new understandings; use tools in strategic ways.

Teacher Tips: Provide a variety of repurposed floorboards and cardboard tubes along with toys that roll. Challenge children to create runs that move objects from one place to another. As they become more experienced using the materials, students can sketch their designs into "architecture notebooks." Educators can nudge children's thinking as they play alongside them, noticing and naming mathematical details of the experience. For example, teachers and students might notice and wonder together about the effect of various sizes and shapes of the tubes: Are the tubes wide enough for an object to pass through? Will they be long enough to

reach another tube so the car or ball doesn't roll off the track? Teachers also might help children problem solve when their plans do not work as anticipated.

Building runs provides multiple opportunities for children to see that learning can be a fluid, messy experience in which mistakes in the design and construction stages make the final product stronger. These playful opportunities to problem solve empower children to take risks and try new approaches in future math work.

FIGURE 5.11
A boy uses long repurposed plastic tubes to transport stones from one area of the playground to another.

OUTDOOR COOKING

Suggested Materials: repurposed pots, pans, muffin tins, spoons, cups, or whisks; water; natural objects (e.g., seeds, twigs, mud); writing materials like paper and crayons; recipe books

What's the Math? Count to tell the number of objects; describe and compare measurable attributes; classify objects and count the number of objects in each category; use tools in strategic ways.

Teacher Tips: Children love to create soups and stews outdoors in "mud kitchens." Even if your schoolyard does not have an outdoor dramatic play area, providing a basket of tubes, funnels, spoons, cups, ladles, whisks, and other cooking tools near a collection of tree stumps, sensory bins, or even a mulch pile will encourage children to dramatize and incorporate math ideas into their play. These objects can also be carried in a basket to a local park or nature area, creating an "on the go" dramatic arts center. As children collect natural objects from the schoolyard (e.g., leaves, acorns, petals), they can also classify and sort them into different bowls or tins.

Children may also want to create their own recipes that incorporate measuring and counting: "I'm adding five acorns for spice into my soup."

"Ten leaves will give my chili lots of flavor." Educators can encourage math conversations through thoughtful questioning: "Tell me about your recipe. What are you cooking? What ingredients did you use? How much of that ingredient did you use? Did you need more grass or more rocks to make that?" Math writing can be encouraged by providing notebooks or a large easel for children to record their recipes and potions. Children may notice connections between their outdoor play-cooking and the math that occurs regularly in their lives, during cooking or grocery shopping with their families, for example.

FIGURE 5.12
A child creates his own "soup" in the mud kitchen by adding twigs, leaves, flower petals, and seeds to water.

OUTDOOR NUMBER LINE

Suggested Materials: sidewalk chalk, natural objects

What's the Math? Know number names and the count sequence; count to tell the number of objects; compare numbers; reason numerically; use tools in strategic ways.

Teacher Tips: Number lines are excellent tools for encouraging children to name and sequence numbers, while providing a model that can be used for early addition and subtraction. They also help children develop number sense as they think about which numbers are close to or far apart from each other. Number lines found on everyday math tools (e.g., rulers) can be offered to children to incorporate into their outdoor play and activities.

Educators can encourage math thinking in children by providing predrawn number lines and observing how children incorporate them into their play. Children may use them to play counting and skipping games (e.g., hopscotch); they may search the schoolyard and place collections on each number (e.g., one stick, two leaves, three rocks); or they may use a number line to measure the length or width of objects (e.g., by lying next to the line to see how tall they are).

Number lines can also be used in response to a child's curiosity about an outdoor object or event. For example, when Cole was curious to see how far he could jump, he used the number line to calculate the length of his jump. His starting position was always on the number one, and after multiple attempts, he was able to reach his personal best by jumping to the number six. As his friends became interested in what he was doing, Cole was able to compare his jumps to theirs, calculating and comparing who had the longest and shortest jump.

FIGURE 5.13
A child incorporates a number line into his outdoor play.

Teacher-Initiated Explorations

Alice and Sam stood together looking at the number cards that had been placed in baskets on the ground. In front of them was a thick piece of yarn I had tied between two posts. The two children emptied the baskets onto the ground and used the large space to spread out the cards so that each number was visible. Alice picked up the card with the number one.

"I think the one goes here." Alice pointed to the end of the yarn closest to the left post. "We start with number one when we count."

Over the next several minutes, the two children worked together to hang the number cards in order on the yarn. As other children noticed their work, they stopped by to see what was happening in this activity. Some skipped along next to the line, reciting the numbers already placed on the yarn and pointing to each one as they passed. Others helped look through the remaining cards still on the ground in search of the numbers needed to complete the sequence. When the children tired of this activity, they removed the numbers from the line and placed them on the ground in front of the yarn.

"Let's see if we can find things to match the numbers!" Sam shouted as he ran toward the garden. "I'm going to pick flowers. You look for something else."

The children searched the garden and grassy area, retrieving different objects and placing them in piles next to the number cards.

"Okay, I've got one rock, so I'm going to put that next to the number one," Alice said. "What did you find?"

The children sorted their objects, counting them out and matching them to the number cards, changing the activity from a number-ordering experience to one focused on exploring collections and quantity.

WHEN A TEACHER brings materials outside with a specific intention, focus, or goal, we refer to these as teacher-initiated explorations (see Figures 5.14, 5.15, and 5.16 for examples). These explorations may include activities, games, or challenges. For example, children might be asked to sort a collection of natural materials using trays, challenged to find a pattern in nature, asked to find the longest crack in the sidewalk, or encouraged to find the heaviest rock to put on a scale. Teachers can create activities such as these that both honor children's developmental stages and interests and connect to program requirements and standards (Leong and Bodrova 2012).

Here are some of our favorite teacher-initiated explorations:

NUMBER LINES

Suggested Materials: yarn, clothespins, subitizing cards (numbers, ten frames, tallies, dots, dice images)

What's the Math? Represent numbers in different ways; compare numbers; use tools in strategic ways.

Teacher Tips: Hang a long piece of yarn between two trees or posts and offer children a basket of subitizing cards and a basket of clothespins. Providing children with a large area in which to work gives them freedom to spread the cards out on the ground in a comfortable fashion. Hanging the yarn between trees that are far apart provides children with a very long number line, something that might not be possible in the classroom space. Encourage children to examine each number card using what they know about different representations of number (e.g., five dots and the numeral 5 are two ways to represent the number five). As children identify the number represented on each card, invite them to clip the card in order on the line. You can prompt children by asking questions: "What number do you see?" "Where do you think that number should be placed on our number line?" "How else might we order the numbers on the line?" As children become comfortable identifying and ordering the numbers, challenge them to consider different ways of placing the cards on the line (e.g., decreasing, skip counting, odd or even numbers).

FIGURE 5.14
Children can notice, classify, and count different objects in the schoolyard. Here, children are encouraged to observe what is in each hoop, recording the name and number of objects found.

FIGURE 5.15
In this teacher-initiated spatial reasoning exploration, children are encouraged to place the pattern blocks within the sections of tape, creating a design that includes rotational symmetry.

FIGURE 5.16
A teacher creates a geometric design using masking tape. Children are then encouraged to color in each section with sidewalk chalk. When the tape is removed, a beautiful geometric design will be revealed. Children can also place the tape in their own geometric designs, focusing on the shapes they create within a certain area.

PATTERNS, PATTERNS EVERYWHERE!

Suggested Materials: pattern photo cards, iPads, other devices with a camera

What's the Math? Recognize, identify, and describe patterns in the natural world.

Teacher Tips: Before inviting children to play this game, explore your outdoor space to find interesting patterns (e.g., bricks on a wall, designs on a sidewalk, lines on a fence). Take photos of the patterns; print and laminate them so they are durable. Photos can be stored on a ring for easy access. When the pattern cards are ready, invite children to use them during outside time. Explain that the patterns are hiding in different places in the outdoor space and that children can use the cards to help them go on a pattern hunt. After some practice, invite children to create their own pattern cards. Bring an iPad or other device with a camera outside and encourage children to take photos of the patterns they discover. These photos can be printed and prepared

for future pattern hunts in the schoolyard. There are many patterns outdoors that are not available inside (e.g., petals on a flower, tread marks on a tire), and a larger space to explore will offer children a different kind of challenge than an indoor pattern search might. Working with patterns helps children see relationships and develop generalizations, preparing them for many kinds of math work, now and later on in their lives.

FIGURE 5.17
A child takes a photo of a pattern she sees on flower buds using a tablet.

NUMBER SCAVENGER HUNT

Suggested Materials: number cards, clipboard, master number list, pencils

What's the Math? Know number names and count sequence; count to tell the number of objects; understand addition as putting together and adding to, and understand subtraction as taking apart and taking from; reason numerically.

Teacher Tips: Before bringing children into the outdoor space, hide various number cards (e.g., 1–10, 1–20). Invite children to go on a number scavenger hunt during outdoor play. Each child will have a clipboard, a list of all the numbers hidden in the yard, and a pencil. As children scout the outdoor space and find the numbers, they can cross them off their list until they have found each one. Increase the number of cards hidden to add a challenge. Children can also be challenged to place collections of natural objects by the number cards as they discover them. For example, they can place one rock by the number 1, two leaves by the number 2, and three sticks by the number 3. Create a different type of scavenger hunt by placing objects by the number cards and encouraging children to find additional objects to add up to that number or to take objects away if too many are present. For example, if a child finds the number 6 and a set of two sticks, she would look for four more sticks to add to the collection. Ask children to suggest other ways of playing addition and subtraction games using the cards and objects found in the school-yard. Children can also go on a neighborhood walk and look for numbers in the world around them (e.g., apartment numbers, street signs). As numbers are located, they can be recorded on a tracking sheet.

Finding useful numbers in the community can lead to discussions about the roles these numbers play. For instance, numbers on buildings help us locate specific places. Speed signs control traffic and keep us safe on a busy street. Number scavenger hunts can help children see the connection between the math they are learning in school and the important role it plays in their everyday lives.

COLOR SORT AND MATCH

Suggested Materials: large color wheel (made by the children or purchased from an art store), natural loose parts (found outside by the children or provided by an educator)

What's the Math? Classify objects and count the number of objects in each category; engage in reasoning and argumentation.

Teacher Tips: Place the color wheel in a central location in the outdoor space. Invite children to search the play area for various natural materials (e.g., flowers, leaves, bark). As children find items, ask them to observe and identify the attributes of each object and place it on the corresponding section of the color wheel. For example, if a leaf has turned red in the fall weather, the child can place the leaf on the red spot on the color wheel. Children may decide that an object fits into more than one color category. Many shades of red also have orange tints, and some shades of green also appear to be blue. Ask children to choose a color for the object and justify their choice. Outdoor space offers many possibilities for finding interesting and colorful objects, especially during seasonal changes. This activity could be repeated each season. Consider taking a photo of each completed color wheel and comparing the objects found in its sections. If your outdoor space doesn't offer enough variety, consider providing objects from different areas—bring some materials from home, or ask families to donate materials from their yards. You could also go on a walk to a nearby park or nature area for a change of scenery.

Children may disagree on where an object should be placed on the color wheel. This activity provides an opportunity for children to articulate the reasoning behind their own choices (e.g., "Even though this leaf has a little orange on it, it's mostly red so it goes on the red part of the wheel.") and listen to the reasoning of their peers. The job of sorting also provides an opportunity for children to grapple with a "problem" to which there are many reasonable solutions. Practicing how to articulate and justify their thinking and how to listen to ideas that are different from their own empowers children, building both the trust they place in their own work and their comfort level with engaging in productive argumentation.

Children's Observations and Wonderings over Time

MANY OUTDOOR inquiries happen in bits and pieces over time. These inquiries often involve a combination of student-initiated noticing and wondering and teacher-initiated activities. Students may have an inquiry they would like to research over the course of several days, such as collecting as many different leaves as they can find and ordering them by size (see Figures 5.18, 5.19, and 5.20). Here are some other math- and science-based questions that students have investigated:

- ◆ Why does the size of my shadow change when I'm outside at different times of day?

- ◆ How long will it take to build the new office building on the end of the block? How deep is the hole they are digging for the foundation?

- ◆ How many trucks drive past our classroom window each hour? Is it the same number every day?

- ◆ How much did it rain this week?

- ◆ Which animals are leaving the different-sized tracks by our playground?

FIGURE 5.18
Our students searched the schoolyard for interesting leaves over the course of several days in the spring. They classified, sorted, and counted what they found.

FIGURE 5.19

Children were fascinated with the formation of leaves on branches. They challenged themselves to find the branch with the most leaves on it.

Teachers can support student-initiated inquiries in a number of ways. They can provide supplemental resources such as books and photos. They can encourage children to represent their ideas using many mediums, such as drawing, writing, and painting. And they can engage children in ongoing conversation and documentation as their ideas and theories evolve over the course of the investigation (Wien and Halls 2018).

Mathematical inquiries are not necessarily planned ahead of time. You may find that you move gradually from more structured or planned activities to more spontaneous explorations of children's wonderings through a mathematical lens. You can begin this process by tuning in to children's wonderings and by spending time observing them as they work and play. Once a mathematical problem or question emerges, you can

FIGURE 5.20

The children created leaf rubbings with white crayon on cardstock and colored over them using watercolors in order to preserve the designs. Once the paint was dry, the children cut out the individual leaves and ordered them on a string according to size.

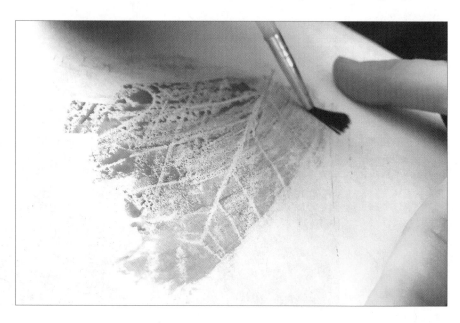

act as a guide, supporting and scaffolding the inquiry (Wien 2014). These inquiries are meaningful regardless of their duration—a group of children might wonder about the changing color of the leaves over the course of several weeks in the fall, or they may have a quick discussion about the hundreds of ants they notice underneath a tree in front of the school.

Here are a few examples of inquiries we have conducted in our outdoor space:

INQUIRY **Winter Bird Count**

As an avid birder myself, I was eager to bring my love of bird feeding and watching to the classroom. One snowy day I hung a feeder just outside our classroom window. Over the course of several days, the children began to notice a variety of species visiting the feeder, including both birds and squirrels. I provided tools and materials near our window to inspire deeper observations, conversation, and thinking about what was happening in our schoolyard. I also added other feeders with different types of seed in each (see Figure 5.21). As birds visited the feeders, the children used binoculars to watch them more closely, looking through our bird guides to identify them, and sketching the different birds they noticed in journals. As more birds came to the feeders,

FIGURE 5.21
Children put out various types of seeds to attract as large a variety of birds as possible to the feeder. Once the birds began visiting, the children recorded how many of each they observed, using tallies on a tracking sheet.

the children began to take turns recording the number of each type of bird they saw. They also collected data on the shape and size of the birds, what type of seed each type of bird preferred, and whether a type of bird visited in the morning or afternoon. After a month of observation, the children compiled their data on chart paper (with adult help), analyzed their findings, and shared their bird research with a local conservatory. ■

INQUIRY Kindergarten Olympics

In our schoolyard, we have a collection of stumps and logs on which children enjoy climbing. These logs can also be turned on their sides and easily rolled around our space, adding variety to the children's play and providing a challenging physical activity. One day I overheard a group of children challenging one another to a race around the stumps. They had noticed the older children practicing in the yard for an upcoming track-and-field day and were interested in having their own races. Curious to see what the children would do next, I placed a basket with a variety of timers (e.g., sand timer, stopwatch, visual timer) next to the stumps during the next outdoor time. The children took immediate notice and experimented with the various timers. After choosing the stopwatch, they began to time themselves maneuvering around the stumps to see who could do it the fastest. Over the next few days, the children worked to create more complex obstacles with the stumps so that the races were more challenging. They even asked for a large easel to be placed next to the finish line so that each racer's name and time could be recorded. ■

INQUIRY City Shapes

Children in one class had been discussing their local community for a few days as part of their social studies unit. As they drew pictures of local landmarks (e.g., the library, community center, subway station) in their journals, they noticed and discussed that many structures were composed of shapes. "The library is a big square! It has lots of little square windows in front," observed one student. "I think that the subway station has an arch that you have to go under when you walk down the stairs. There are lots of little rectangle tiles on it that are different colors," said another. These wonderings inspired their teacher to consider how he might plan a walking field trip around their neighborhood for later in the week. Maybe the children could bring clipboards and draw the shapes they observed in buildings or track how many of each shape they found along the way. Or perhaps the teacher or parent volunteers could take photos of the buildings for children to analyze and recreate using the wooden blocks in the construction center. ■

Building, Displaying, and Exploring Collections

CHILDREN LOVE trinkets and treasures—feathers, stones, shells, nests, leaves. They love to sort and count what they collect, often using familiar classroom tools such as ten frames and hundred charts to organize their count. In our classroom, these collections fill clear jars and line shelves. They are also offered in wicker baskets during outdoor play. In addition to supplementing our classroom resources and beautifying our space, these loose parts are integral play props that the children use

FIGURE 5.22
Objects from nature are displayed in jars on a shelf at children's height. Mirrors placed behind reflect the objects and natural lighting in the room.

for a variety of purposes. They can be used as they are or reimagined into something else. For example, crushed dried leaves become spices used in recipes in the mud kitchen; a piece of driftwood becomes a phone. The arrival of each season brings opportunities to find new collections. We often recruit families for assistance and ask that they search their own yards and neighborhoods to help supplement our collection. Older children in the school are also eager to share their discoveries with our classroom. One year we had a collection of live spiders in jars, including a wolf spider, and witnessed babies emerging from her egg sack and clinging to her back. (Some of our collections tend to be kept for rather short periods of time!)

Curating collections of natural items is an easy and cost-effective way to both integrate math into outdoor play and bring parts of the outside world into our classroom math experiences. Children can notice and name common characteristics and sort objects based on a variety of attributes—type of object, material, size, color, shape, smell, touch. Loose parts can be used to create geometric and symmetrical designs in the art center, placed on the light table for shadow play, or incorporated into the building center.

Getting Started with Outdoor Math

MANY EDUCATORS appreciate the need for children to spend large blocks of uninterrupted time playing outside. In our program, we spend a minimum of one hour outdoors each day, rain or shine, and encourage children to dress for the weather. This chapter, however, is written with both longer and shorter outdoor mathematical explorations in mind. Outdoor learning time can be effective even if it occurs only every few days or for shorter durations. I have also found that teachers who begin with shorter periods of outdoor math work often become committed to expanding the time and ways in which children are able to work outdoors.

Sharing the rationale for our outdoor work throughout the school year is important for bringing administrators, colleagues, and families

FIGURE 5.23
The changing of the seasons offers new and interesting ways to rediscover the same space throughout the school year. These children run through a cornfield located near their school after the harvest has ended.

onboard as partners and for building understanding and trust in the work we do. Sharing research-based evidence for the importance of outdoor play and communicating children's experiences using photo and video documentation can help make visible the rich learning happening outside.

Common concerns about outdoor learning can be addressed with respectful communication. For example, children are often a bit disheveled after exploring outdoor spaces. Some families may find this disconcerting. We explain to them that messiness is often a sign of hard work for young children. We also encourage them to prepare their children for our work outdoors by dressing them appropriately for the weather. Laying this groundwork has helped us avoid difficult conversations at dismissal time. Even with this preparation, however, some children may arrive at school unprepared for the day's weather. Having a large basket of gently used outerwear (e.g., raincoats, boots, mittens) helps us include all children in our outdoor learning. These materials have been donated by families, provided by the PTA, and collected by staff from secondhand stores. Ensuring that every child is prepared to play outside is a priority. Over time, many families and schools realize that outdoor exploration naturally complements children's mathematical thinking. Being attuned to the children's observations, helping to recognize their questions and highlight the math within them, and supporting nature-based inquiries make this learning meaningful.

If your school does not offer regular outdoor time, consider what opportunities in your schedule there might be for taking children's learning outside. Perhaps a lesson on seasonal changes might be the spark you need to head into your neighborhood for a fall walk, integrating math whenever possible. Perhaps there is a local park, farmers' market, or other outdoor space close by that you could travel to on occasion. Can your gym class happen in the schoolyard and incorporate math ideas too? Even opening a classroom window can connect children with the outdoors.

Not All Classrooms Have Four Walls

Outdoor spaces are unique; some schools have large treed areas, bountiful gardens, and a diverse ecosystem with insects and animals to discover. Other schools' outdoor spaces are simpler, with patches of grassy space or asphalt blacktops. Some schools are located in busy urban centers with community parks, markets, and gardens a short walking distance away. Others are on the edges of fields surrounded by crops, barns, and orchards. Different kinds of outdoor spaces can offer a wealth of math learning for children. Look at the potential of your outdoor space through a mathematical lens.

FIGURE 5.24
Subway and bus maps offer opportunities for math exploration. Children can count how many stops there are before their destination, predict how long a ride might be, estimate how many passengers are on their train, or help calculate the total cost for a ride.

These questions might help to facilitate your reflection on your school's outdoor space:

- ◆ Which type of activities would be easiest to implement in your space and help guide you on your journey?

- ◆ What aspects of the outdoor space do you already appreciate?

- ◆ Are there easy and cost-effective changes that can enhance what you already have?

- ◆ Are there areas available for storage of materials if items cannot be left unattended overnight?

- ◆ Would your school community be willing to donate financial or volunteer support for projects to enhance the outdoor space?

- ◆ Are there outdoor education grants you can access through your school district or community?

- ◆ Can found and repurposed objects (tree stumps, tires, large stones, logs) be placed in outdoor areas to add layers and encourage big body exploration as children line up objects by size, roll them into position to help define a space, challenge themselves to see how far they can jump, or create timed obstacle courses through which to maneuver?

- ◆ Can sensory tables or contained sensory areas be created or moved into the spaces during outdoor play that contain messy materials such as sand, water, pea stone, and other inviting materials?

- ◆ What aspects of your overall curriculum naturally integrate well with the outdoors? Are there certain subject areas or concepts that can be explored in the outdoor space? How might you tie outdoor learning to your standards and goals?

- ◆ What support do you have for outdoor programming? How might you articulate the importance of outdoor learning to families and other educational stakeholders? Can you partner with another class in your grade or district to make outdoor learning more manageable and effective?

Enhancing the Space You Have

Creating outdoor math opportunities doesn't have to be expensive or complicated. Small changes can inspire big results in children's (and educators'!) math experiences outdoors. Over time, you'll see your outdoor space transform as you add repurposed and donated objects and create nooks for various experiences. One potential first step is the addition of sensory areas. If you do not have space or resources to install a permanent sand or water feature in your outdoor area, you can wheel indoor sand and water tables outside when weather permits. For those who would rather not transport bulky sensory tables, even simple bins filled with water can be placed on outdoor tables, stumps, or even the ground. These arrangements encourage math conversation as children experiment and problem solve with sensory materials.

If you are limited by your space, seek nearby substitutes instead. Going on a weekly community walk around the neighborhood or visiting a nearby green space on a regular basis are good alternatives. Perhaps there is a nature trail within walking distance of your school, or the children in your community live on farms that border your school. Invite families to suggest different spaces to explore and to join in on the math exploration—not only will they provide extra support, but you can pair them with children and suggest a mathematical conversation starter to enhance their walk: "Can you find the numbers one to ten?" "What shapes do you recognize?" "How long will it take until we get there?" "How many different signs can you spot?" "How fast do you think those cars are driving?"

Field trips also offer opportunities for math learning. A visit to an apple orchard or pumpkin patch can provide opportunities for children to think about the mathematics of growing food. On a walk to the local library, you might ask children to predict the number of cars and trucks they will see along the way. Bring clipboards and pencils so they can keep track using a T-chart.

When visiting a sugar bush, the children in our class wondered how many drops of syrup it would take to fill a bucket. This question sparked a number talk, integrating what the children knew about number relationships and measurement. Upon returning to our classroom we displayed a photo of the bucket along with writing materials, water, a bucket, and droppers, and encouraged the children to see if they could estimate and then prove how many drops it would take.

FIGURE 5.25

A fall trip to the farm is full of math potential as children count and compare different sizes and shapes of trees, pumpkins, and apples.

On field trips, consider allowing children to take photographs of things they find interesting, so that these can be printed and examined once the children have returned to school. Perhaps reviewing the photos during whole-group time will elicit an observation or question that can be explored further. For example, a photo of a tractor pulling a wagon of pumpkins might inspire children to wonder just how many pumpkins are being pulled. Think beyond the schoolyard when evaluating mathematically rich places for children to explore.

Exploring the math that can be found just beyond our classroom windows and doors can spark joy for teachers and children alike. Outdoor experiences help children view math more broadly and connect what they learn inside the classroom with the wider world.

Documentation is not pretty pictures of engaged children. Rather, it captures the thinking process: What motivated [students] to begin, continue, change direction? What were the breakthroughs, the pivotal remarks or actions? How did they solve the problem?
—ANN LEWIN-BENHAM

CHAPTER 6

Using Documentation to Honor Children's Math Experiences

FIGURE 6.1

A child reviews the artifacts placed in his personal learning journal.

Grabbing his learning journal from a low shelf, Finn plopped down in an oversized chair next to Rose and opened the journal in his lap. He pointed to a photo on one of his pages.

"Look! There's me!" Finn beamed. "I'm building something! My tower is so tall. I used so many blocks!"

Rose nodded. "Yeah, I like to build too. But look at my picture." Rose pointed to a photo in her journal. "In this one someone was measuring how tall I was with a piece of string. Look how small it is. I was little then."

"I was little then too, but I'm bigger now," Finn replied.

"I'm bigger too!" Rose agreed.

"I can build an even taller building! I'm going to use one hundred blocks this time!" Finn returned his journal to the shelf and set off for the building center, determined to create a larger structure than the one in his journal.

"Wait!" Rose called out behind him. "I can measure how tall your building is if I can find a piece of string!"

What Is Documentation and Why Does It Matter?

DOCUMENTATION IS the process of gathering and reflecting on evidence and artifacts from children's experiences in the classroom. This process serves as a way of honoring and recording children's lived experiences and making their learning visible to each other, educators, families, and the greater community (Rinaldi 2006). Educators use the documentation process as a form of assessment, taking note of what children understand and planning for next steps forward in instruction.

In our classroom, documentation is a living part of our community. Children's work and thinking are posted on classroom walls, recorded in journals, and shared with families. Children, like Finn and Rose in the opening vignette, often review the documentation throughout the classroom, both to reflect on their past learning and to inspire new ideas and questions they want to explore. Documentation helps families and other visitors to our classroom connect the learning they see happening in front of them to the learning that has happened in the classroom over time. This is especially important because much of what young children do in the classroom is process-based and does not always result in a finished product to display. For example, over many days, during choice time, children in our classroom explored perimeter and area by filling different-sized frames with square carpet tiles. They investigated a variety of questions: "Will this long skinny rectangle frame fit more squares inside of it than this small square one?" "How many squares do I need to fill the entire frame?" "Which frame will need the most squares to fill it?" (See Figure 6.2.) When children tired of this activity, they moved on to using more challenging pentomino pieces, trying to leave no empty spaces in between (see Figure 6.3). All this thinking

FIGURE 6.2
A child explores the concept of area by filling a frame with repurposed carpet squares.

FIGURE 6.3
A child fills the area of a frame using pentominoes, attempting to leave no empty spaces between pieces.

would have been lost as we cleaned up at the end of the day had we not planned for documentation. Using photos and recording students' questions, the children and I created documentation that allowed them to revisit their ideas, allowed me to assess their learning, and allowed visitors to access children's thinking even if they weren't there when it was happening.

Documenting children's mathematical experiences serves several important purposes:

◆ **Documentation communicates the value of children's ideas and work.** When we record children's words, take photos of their work, and then share these words and photos in some form, we send the message that children's ideas are worthy of consideration by their classmates, teachers, school communities, and others.

FIGURE 6.4
Proud of his work, a child asked to write to his family about fitting pattern blocks into a tray.

◆ **Documentation offers a glimpse into children's learning over time and allows children to reflect on their own ongoing learning.** Depending on its format, documentation may provide a record of children's thinking in a single moment or over a period of time. Think back to the opening vignette. When Finn reviewed the photos of his building projects from earlier in the school year, he recognized his previous accomplishment (building a tall tower) but also how much he had grown in his thinking and strategies. Looking at the photos inspired Finn to revisit a question ("How can I build a tall tower?") with new strategies and ideas. Figure 6.5 provides another example of how we might document a child's learning over time. This photo shows the progression of one child's ability to represent still life artistically over time.

◆ **Documentation helps children make connections between their own ideas and work and those of their classmates.** As children review artifacts of their learning, they can notice similarities and differences between their own ideas and their classmates' ideas. They can build on each other's ideas through working together and on their own. After Rose and Finn explored two separate learning experiences in their journals (Finn's tall tower and Rose being measured with string), they made connections between the two events and decided to work together on a new task.

◆ **Documentation allows teachers to reflect on children's learning and plan next steps for instruction.** Children can be encouraged

FIGURE 6.5
These three pieces show how one child progressed in making still life artwork. Displaying her creations in the order in which they were created draws attention to the ways she has learned to represent detail and portray what she observes using a variety of artistic mediums.

to share their ideas in many different ways. As educators curate this information, they can look for trends in the data. Their observations may help them uncover what children know and enjoy about a certain topic and what they might be ready for next. For example, some students have many strategies for addition of smaller numbers, but they may tend to rely on Unifix cubes when working with larger numbers. The documentation may reveal that some children are ready to explore place value with manipulatives.

◆ **Documentation engages families and the greater community with students' experiences in the classroom.** Documentation is a bridge between families and classrooms, allowing families to understand their children's learning even if they were not there in the moment it occurred. Often, documentation helps families emotionally connect with their children's success at school, providing images, for example, of children's triumphant reactions when they have created a complex pattern or solved a difficult problem. This connection helps to build families' trust and support for the work going on in the classroom. Documentation can also invite families to bring their knowledge to the classroom. For instance, after studying patterns found in nature, children in our class shared photos of their work with their families and invited them to search their yards and neighborhoods for additional patterns to be explored later by the class. Documentation can also provide families with specific information about how to support their children's learning at home. For example, documents showcasing a child's journey exploring the composition of numbers helps a family better understand how to reinforce this learning over the summer break.

◆ **Documentation helps children share their learning beyond the walls of the school, with the greater community.** When appropriate, it can be powerful to share documentation of children's learning in the community. This helps connect the neighborhood to the local school as children's learning is incorporated into local institutions such as libraries, stores, parks, and centers. One year, the children in my class wanted to help a food bank that was running low on food. They created a documentation panel showcasing past food drives that had been held at our school and the many ways students had calculated the number of items the class had collected over time. We then asked the manager of the local grocery store if we could post our documentation near their food pantry collection bin. Our hope was that our panel would draw attention to the collection bin and inspire shoppers to contribute items after they had perused and appreciated our math work. Another time, the children were eager to share their artwork with visitors to the school. During a "Meet the Teacher" barbecue, we displayed their paintings on the wooden fence so that they could be enjoyed during the evening's festivities (see Figure 6.6).

How Can We Document Children's Mathematical Experiences?

WE CAN MAKE children's thinking visible through photos, videos, and transcripts of children's conversations. Documentation allows us to tell the story of the mathematical thinking occurring in our classrooms. Let's

FIGURE 6.6
Children's paintings are displayed on a fence during a community event being held in the schoolyard.

take a look at several ways we can document children's mathematical work in the classroom and share this work both within our classroom communities and beyond.

Observation as Documentation

One June, the children in our classroom spent several days creating marble runs from pool noodles in our building center. They noticed that the higher they held the noodles, the steeper the incline would be and the faster the marbles would travel. After watching them work, I wondered what they would do if we brought the materials outside. This exploration required a lot of space, and I felt the children were limited in our building center. I also knew that sometimes children who shied away from group activities in the noisy building center would participate in such activities in the open air.

That afternoon we headed outside. Along with the pool noodles and marbles, I also brought rolls of colorful duct tape. I watched as individual children grabbed a few pool noodles each. They easily attached them together, creating a longer run for their marbles (see Figure 6.7). However, the children became frustrated when they realized that there weren't more noodles to add to their creations. So many children were participating in the activity that that we had run out. Curious about how they would solve this problem, I stepped back and watched. I wondered whether the students would realize that working together would allow them access to more noodles. We had built with straws and connectors a few weeks earlier and I anticipated a few might recall this experience and make a connection to their current work. I also was curious to see whether any child would emerge as a leader, directing the others in their building endeavors. A few moments passed. Some children were content to play with their short marble runs and stayed in their places on the asphalt. Two children became frustrated with the activity and walked away, leaving their partially completed runs on the ground.

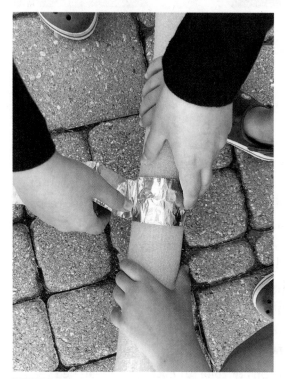

FIGURE 6.7
Children use duct tape to connect pool noodles in order to create a large marble run outdoors.

"Hey, look!" Matek called to his friend. "Brynn left her noodles. We can use them."

"Yeah," Zavier responded. "Let's connect them to ours." Matek and Zavier worked together. After taping Brynn's noodles to theirs, they had a very long marble run. Other children took notice.

"How did you do that?" Karrie asked. "I want a long marble run too!"

"Then just add yours to ours," answered Zavier.

"No, I don't want to give you my noodles," Karrie frowned. "That's not fair."

"You're not giving us your noodles, silly," Matek explained. "You're adding yours to ours. We're sharing. We can make a really long marble run this way!" The three children worked together to attach Karrie's noodles. Other children came over to watch.

"Hey, if we put them all together, maybe they'll reach across the blacktop!" Karrie yelled to a group standing by her. "We can work on it together."

I jotted my observations in a notebook. I made sure to record a few quotes from their conversation to add to a photo of their finished marble run. I was curious to see whether the children would continue to use all the pool noodles to create the longest marble run possible. What would they do when the noodles ran out again? I also noted a shift in the way some children were collaborating. Earlier in the year, Matek might have stomped off if someone had challenged him with "I don't want to give you my noodles." Now he was able to explain his plan better and try to convince his classmate to join him rather than getting upset. I planned to ask the children about their experience collaborating during our whole-group conversation.

THE HEART of successful documentation is observation. When teachers focus on listening to children as they play and work, they avoid taking over children's learning. Rinaldi (2006) reminds us, however, that even observation is not without bias and judgment. In fact, as we watch children closely, we are already forming a relationship with them—connecting with what we are seeing, forming opinions about what the child might already know, and planning for how to move forward in order to best support learning. It's important to recognize that we have biases and individual perspectives when we observe children, causing us sometimes to misinterpret or misrepresent children's actions and words. The process of documentation allows us to return to an experience long after it has passed and reflect upon something we might have missed in the moment. Also, having a large collection of documentation helps us see trends in the data and more accurately judge what a child knows and can do. In these ways, documentation can help us address and confront our own biases.

Many educators use anecdotal notes to help clarify their observations and quickly record what they observe in activities. I often capture math learning using photos and then add anecdotal notes when I can. These annotated photos are more layered than anecdotal notes alone. The photo reveals things that my words may not. For example, a child's face shows emotions she may have been feeling in the moment, and the photo's background often shows interesting details not noticed at the time the photo was taken. Photos of children engaged in math can also be an effective tool for family engagement, especially for those caregivers who might not have had positive experiences themselves with math in school.

Student Work as Documentation

Ben and Ethan are both kindergarten teachers in the same school. Although they each have their own class, they often work together to analyze student work and plan instruction. One afternoon, Ben and Ethan spread out documentation collected from the previous week. On the large table in front of them are photos of children working and playing, children's drawings, and their own notes from working alongside their students. As they discuss each piece of evidence, the two teachers notice that many children have been exploring patterns during choice time. This is a snapshot of some of their conversation:

> **Ben:** So, I noticed that the children seemed to be really interested in patterns this week. In this photo, Emily created a pattern using the links. She continued her pattern all the way across the table. And Quinn drew buildings that seemed to be in a pattern formation. (See Figure 6.8.)

FIGURE 6.8
A child writes about patterning in his journal.

Ethan: Huh, that's interesting. We've had links out all month and no one has made patterns with them. They have mostly been interested in using them to measure each other's height.

Ben: I have a small group of children who always choose to make patterns in our room. They seem to see patterns everywhere! When we read *The Very Hungry Caterpillar* yesterday, Sawyer noticed that the book has a pattern. The number of each food item the caterpillar ate was growing by one. I introduced the term "growing patterns" to the students in that group and they were really interested in recreating *The Very Hungry Caterpillar* pattern with blocks.

Ethan: Hmm! I never thought to look for patterns in stories. I wonder if I read the book to my group whether they would see something similar. Have you seen how the children in my class love to build with the little wooden cubes? Recently, they were working on building staircases. I wonder if we can connect their interest in building with their interest in patterns. Maybe we can put out an invitation to build growing patterns with cubes next week.

As Ben and Ethan continue to review the documentation together, they discuss what they notice, paying careful attention to each other's interpretations of each artifact. They know that each person brings their own perspectives and biases to the table when analyzing student work and have learned that their collaboration helps them understand their respective students in new and deeper ways. This discussion helps Ben and Ethan see how connected the children's playful explorations are to the math curriculum. Additionally, the two teachers work together to consider next steps for learning and possible lessons and activities they might use with their students.

Documentation Throughout the Classroom

Documentation is a living, organic part of our classroom. In addition to children's individual portfolios, we keep collections of evidence throughout our space, housed on clipboards, placed in binders, posted

FIGURE 6.9
A child takes photos of pumpkins using a tablet during a measurement activity. The photo will be printed and added to a cumulative documentation display in the classroom.

on walls, and sprinkled throughout learning centers. This documentation helps share, honor, and celebrate the rich learning that happens over time. Many of the children's playful activities are process-based, with little or no final product to share as evidence of learning with families and other stakeholders (e.g., building a large tower using blocks, dissecting a flower with tweezers, testing whether a handmade boat floats in the water table, exploring symmetry with pattern blocks). Activities that do result in a finished piece often are sent home with children at the end of the school day (e.g., drawings, paintings, writing), as children are eager to share their creations with their families. Sometimes children work

FIGURE 6.10
Photo collages are housed on clipboards in each learning center throughout classroom. The documentation here tells the story of the children's explorations during outside time and is displayed in an area of the classroom where many natural loose parts from the outdoors are available for exploration.

The children are exploring the characteristics of buttons in a collection. They use sorting hoops to create a VENN diagram. This is a transcript of their conversation.

Cheyenne: These are all round.

Jamie: I see two different colors—blue and black.

Oliver: I think that the small ones should go together.

Poppy: But there are big ones too.

Oliver: So, put the big ones together on one side and the small ones together on the other side.

Eve: But aren't we supposed to put different ones in different hoops?

Wyn: Where are the medium ones?

Cheyenne: There aren't any medium ones. Only small and big ones.

Eve: Then we should put the small ones on one side and big ones on the other side.

Oliver: That's what I said to do.

Marius: I'm going to check the button container and see what other ones are in there.

FIGURE 6.11

A transcript of a conversation between children is displayed alongside the buttons they used in a sorting activity. The photo inspires children to revisit past ideas, while the transcript allows visiting adults to understand the kind of learning children engage in.

collaboratively in groups on large-scale explorations that are difficult to document for each student individually. By curating documentation over the course of the school year, we can reflect as a group on what has been explored and learned in different classroom areas.

Pedagogical Documentation

As educators collect and organize documentation in the classroom, we strive to engage in a "pedagogy of listening" (Gandini and Kaminsky 2004). When we listen to children's theories about the world around them, we delve more deeply into understanding how they observe and interpret that world. Through this approach, educators become researchers, looking closely and carefully at student artifacts and experiences, using them as a way to guide movement forward while honoring past experiences. Documentation helps us see children in ways that traditional assessment strategies may not. We are able to learn about children as mathematicians and plan learning experiences according to their interests, strengths, and needs. Pedagogical documentation invites student voice as children analyze and craft the stories of their experiences and learning together with educators. In our room, we create and share pedagogical documentation in a variety of ways. Here are some of the methods we have explored:

◆ **Documentation Panels** are displays of various forms of documentation, woven together with educator and student voice. Photos, artwork, transcripts of conversations, reflective writing, and connections to child development or standards of practice can be included. These panels can be placed on classroom walls so that children and visitors can refer to them for information about classroom learning. I usually create a documentation panel for the current math project we are undertaking, in order to highlight our experiences and plan for ways to move forward.

◆ **Photo Collages** are an effective way to quickly share information about a smaller experience or project. Many different apps can be used to create collages digitally, and anecdotal notes and other evidence can be included. Collages allow us to share learning without the time commitment larger documentation panels might require (see Figure 6.10).

◆ **Clipboard Portfolios** are another effective way to organize and present documentation that is subject or center specific. At each classroom center (e.g., art, drama, writing), we have a clipboard that holds various pieces of evidence that have been collected from that area over time. The clipboard portfolio may include photo collages, student artifacts, or questions for children and adults to engage with. Clipboard portfolios allow the lived experiences at the center to be represented (see Figure 6.12).

FIGURE 6.12
A collage that tells a learning story about a specific child's classroom experience is placed alongside materials in the art center.

◆ **Class Books** can be made from paper or digitally using a story maker app. Class books contain photos and narrative to describe the journey that children have taken in arriving at a solution or an answer to a particular inquiry or question. These books can be added to documentation panels as supplemental information, shared in learning centers around the classroom, or shared digitally in student portfolios.

FIGURE 6.13
This QR code links to an iMovie about a project in our classroom.

◆ **iMovies** can tell the story of an experience or inquiry. iMovies can be used as digital documentation panels, in which photos, videos, interviews, and other artifacts of learning can be integrated together in a sequential way, telling the story of an experience or inquiry to an audience (see Figure 6.13).

Getting Started with Documentation

THERE ARE MANY approaches to documenting students' learning in ways that honor their understandings and nudge them to consider new ideas. As you reflect on the role of documentation in your classroom, the following ideas may help you get started with new forms of documentation or build on your existing practices.

Have a plan in place.

Spend time familiarizing yourself with the many different ways observation and documentation can be collected and used to inform student growth and learning. If you assign children grades, consider how you will calculate a final grade for the unit based on the collection of artifacts you will be gathering for each child. Be clear and consistent in your communication so that children and their families are kept informed about the child's current math achievements and what next steps need to be taken in order to promote steady progress.

Be clear about your intentions.

Help children, their families, and your colleagues understand why you are using documentation to provide feedback. Communicate that student growth is the intention behind this choice and that rich, descriptive feedback, along with other forms of assessment, will be provided to help advance children's learning. Be sure to emphasize that observation and documentation help to personalize the learning experience and that feedback will be tailored to each child's interests, strengths, needs, and next steps.

Set clear learning goals and objectives for students.

At the beginning of a new unit of study, set clear learning goals and objectives for students. Keep a running written record of these, adding new items as appropriate, and keep this record posted in a visible place for all learners, perhaps next to documentation displays. Refer regularly to these goals and objectives in order to highlight key concepts and provide guidance and direction for children.

Involve students in the assessment process.

Children can be encouraged to self-assess their work in a unit of study. Take time to meet with each child in order to review the artifacts that have been collected over time. Focus on the areas of strength in each piece, ask the child for their opinions, and suggest next steps for learning. Older children can be asked to self-grade. You can then compare the child's assessment of their learning to your own thinking on how their understanding has grown. Share exemplars of work with the child, reference the goals and objectives outlined at the beginning of the unit, and be honest with your feedback.

Include families in the documentation process.

Families can be empowered to share their observations, understandings, and suggestions for next steps as collaborators in the assessment process. In our classroom, documentation is shared with families using a variety of formats—copies of learning stories, annotated photos, journals, and portfolios are sent home regularly. Families are invited to review the documentation with their children and then communicate their observations and their ideas for supporting their children at home. Sometimes a form with specific prompts is included with the documentation (e.g., What do you notice about your child's learning? What questions do you have for the child or teacher about their work?). Other times families are invited to comment directly on the digital artifact included in the child's portfolio. The information families share helps me to understand the children from a different perspective. Research indicates that children perform better in school when their families are involved in their

FIGURE 6.14
A father visits his son's school to learn about his day.

education. Families that are kept informed about their children's progress are better able to support their children's needs, and informed conversations with teachers support this reciprocal relationship (Ontario Ministry of Education 2016b).

Educators who experiment with diverse, nontraditional ways of observing, documenting, and representing learning in the classroom are making a statement about what they value in children's mathematical journeys. Focusing on the process of learning and not overemphasizing the final product sends the message to children that their developing thinking is what matters the most. Providing descriptive feedback through a variety of tools and formats helps children reflect on their learning. However, students and families are not the only ones who benefit from the focus on observation and documentation. Educators may just find that they grow as much as the children, because the documentation process requires them to continually reflect upon and refine their own practice and mathematical understanding.

Conclusion: Tomorrow's Math—Thinking Back and Thinking Ahead

It was the end of outdoor time and in the corner of the yard I spotted Kace slouched down next to a puddle. Tears ran down his face as he held parts of a boat in his hands. As I approached, I overheard Nyah speaking softly to him.

"It's okay, Kace, whatever is wrong. It's okay. I'll help you," she whispered.

I slowed my step. Wanting to learn what was happening, and curious about Nyah's comforting words, I waited before intervening.

Nyah put her arm around Kace. "Why are you crying? What happened?"

"It's my boat." Kace wiped his eyes. "It won't float. I've worked this whole time and it didn't turn out. Everyone else had one that worked, but not me."

"That's okay," Nyah answered. "I'll help you make one."

"It's too late. Mrs. McLennan blew the whistle. It's time to go home."

"It's never too late!" Nyah reminded him. "We always have tomorrow!"

TWO THINGS stood out to me that day and have stayed with me long after the moment in which they occurred—Kace's persistence in trying to make his boat work until the very last moment before he needed to return indoors, and Nyah's urge to console Kace and help him feel successful. Later that day, as the children were leaving, I watched Kace and Nyah walk out to the bus together. Nyah's boat was in Kace's hand. She had given it to him.

As educators, we often feel like we are running short on time. We may wonder, "With everything else we have to do, do we have time for play?" In her book *Teaching with Intention*, Debbie Miller writes that we can create classrooms in which "no one is looking at the clock; there's not a hint of rush. There's simply the luscious feeling of endless time" (2008, 13). We can create this "luscious feeling of endless time" for what we believe is most important. We can take time to sit beside children and listen to their ideas and questions, challenge them with our own questions, and help them explore the world through mathematics. By giving children this time and attention, we value them not only as mathematical thinkers but as people. And hopefully, we teach them to care in this way for one another.

As you have read this book, I hope you have had an opportunity to reflect on your own classroom community and teaching practice and to see where more moments of joyful math might be sparked. In the opening pages, I asked you to consider the special interests and talents you bring to your teaching practice each day. Now that you've considered the many ways math can be expressed, reflect once more on these interests and talents through a mathematical lens. What next steps might you take toward creating a classroom full of mathematical joy? Be bold, take risks, learn from mistakes, grow your mindset, laugh along the way, and share your ideas far and wide. Tomorrow's math is the evolution of today's joyful ideas.

References

Aspinall, Brian. 2017. *Code Breakers: Increase Creativity, Remix Assessment, and Develop a Class of Coder Ninjas!* San Diego, CA: Dave Burgess Consulting.

Boaler, Jo. 2016. *Mathematical Mindsets: Understanding Students' Potential Through Creative Math, Inspiring Messages and Innovative Teaching.* San Francisco: Jossey-Bass.

Burns, Marilyn. 2005. "3 Lessons by Marilyn Burns: Using Storybooks to Teach Math." *Scholastic Instructor* 114 (7): 27–30.

Dietze, Beverlie, and Diane Kashin. 2019. *Playing and Learning in Early Childhood Education.* 2nd ed. North York, ON: Pearson.

Edwards, Carolyn, Lella Gandini, and George Forman. 1998. *The Hundred Languages of Children: The Reggio Emilia Approach—Advanced Reflections.* 2nd ed. Westport, CT: Ablex.

Gandini, Lella, Lynn Hill, Louise Cadwell, and Charles Schwall, eds. 2005. *In the Spirit of the Studio: Learning from the Atelier of Reggio Emilia.* New York: Teachers College Press.

Gandini, Lella, and Judith Allen Kaminsky. 2004. "Reflections on the Relationship Between Documentation and Assessment in the American Context: An Interview with Brenda Fyfe." *Innovations in Early Education: The International Reggio Exchange*, 11(1), 5–17.

Haury, David L. 2001. *Literature-Based Mathematics in Elementary School.* Washington, DC: National Association for Gifted Children.

Keats, Ezra Jack. 1976. *The Snowy Day.* New York: Puffin Books.

Leong, Deborah J., and Elena Bodrova. 2012. "Assessing and Scaffolding Make-Believe Play." *Young Children* 67 (1): 28–34.

Martin, Bill, Jr., and John Archambault. 1989. *Chicka Chicka Boom Boom.* New York: Birch Lane Books.

McClure, Elisabeth. 2017. "More Than a Foundation: Young Children Are Capable STEM Learners." *Young Children* 72 (5): 83–89.

McDonald, Patricia. 2018. "Observing, Planning, Guiding: How an Intentional Teacher Meets Standards Through Play." *Young Children* 73 (1).

McLennan, Deanna Pecaski. 2018. "The Beautiful Tree Project: Exploring Measurement in Nature." *Teaching Children Mathematics* 25 (1): 16–23.

Miller, Debbie. 2008. *Teaching with Intention: Defining Beliefs, Aligning Practice, Taking Action.* Portsmouth, NH: Stenhouse.

Mraz, Kristine, Alison Porcelli, and Cheryl Tyler. 2016. *Purposeful Play: A Teacher's Guide to Igniting Deep and Joyful Learning Across the Day.* Portsmouth, NH: Heinemann.

Munsch, Robert. 2009. *The Paper Bag Princess.* Toronto, ON: Scholastic.

Ontario Ministry of Education. 2016a. *Growing Success: The Kindergarten Addendum; Assessment, Evaluation, and Reporting in Ontario Schools.* Toronto: Queen's Printer for Ontario.

———. 2016b. *The Kindergarten Program.* Toronto: Queen's Printer for Ontario.

Parker, John. 1988. *I Love Spiders.* New York: Scholastic.

Parrish, Sherry. 2010. *Number Talks: Helping Children Build Mental Math and Computation Strategies.* Sausalito, CA: Math Solutions.

———. 2011. "Number Talks Build Numerical Reasoning: Strengthen Accuracy, Efficiency, and Flexibility with These Mental Math and Computation Strategies." *Teaching Children Mathematics* 18 (3): 198–206.

Pelo, Ann. 2007. *The Language of Art: Inquiry-Based Studio Practices in Early Childhood Settings.* St. Paul, MN: Redleaf Press.

Rinaldi, Carlina. 2006. *In Dialogue with Reggio Emilia: Listening, Researching, and Learning.* New York: Routledge.

Wien, Carol Anne. 2014. *The Power of Emergent Curriculum: Stories from Early Childhood Settings.* Washington, DC: National Association for the Education of Young Children.

Wien, Carol Anne, and Deborah Halls. 2018. "Is There a Chick in There? Kindergartners' Changing Thoughts on Life in an Egg." *Young Children* 73 (1). https://www.naeyc.org/resources/pubs/yc/mar2018/kindergartners-changing-thoughts-life-egg.

Wurm, Julianne P. 2005. *Working in the Reggio Way: A Beginner's Guide for American Teachers.* St. Paul, MN: Redleaf Press.